On the Road: A Guide to Building a Successful Truck Freight Business

Content

Chapter 1

Introduction

The Foundations of a Successful Trucking Business: Laying the Groundwork for Growth

Starting a successful trucking business is not easy, but it can be very rewarding if you're willing to put in the effort. A successful trucking business requires more than just a truck and a driver, it requires a solid foundation that lays the groundwork for growth. In this chapter, we'll take a detailed look at the key elements that are essential for a successful trucking business.

Business Plan

One of the first things you need to do when starting a trucking business is to create a business plan. A business plan is a roadmap that outlines the goals, objectives, and strategies for your business. It should include a detailed description of your business, target market, financial projections, and marketing strategies. Your business plan will be the foundation of your business and will guide your decision-making processes.

Choosing the Right Legal Structure

The legal structure of your trucking business is critical to its success. You need to choose a structure that is suitable for your business needs and provides the right amount of protection for your personal assets. The most common legal structures for trucking businesses are sole proprietorships, partnerships, and limited liability companies (LLCs). Each structure has its pros and cons, and it's important to consult with an attorney or accountant to determine which structure is right for your business.

Getting Your Operating Authority

To operate a trucking business, you need to obtain operating authority from the Federal Motor Carrier Safety Administration (FMCSA). Your operating authority is a license that allows you to operate as a for-hire carrier, and it's essential to have in order to legally transport goods for other businesses. The application process can be lengthy, so it's important to start the process as soon as possible to avoid any delays in getting your business up and running.

Acquiring the Right Equipment

One of the most significant expenses for a trucking business is acquiring the right equipment. You need to purchase or lease a truck that's suitable for the type of freight you plan to transport. It's important to research different types of trucks and equipment to find the best fit for your business needs. You should also consider the age and condition of the equipment, as well as the cost of maintenance and repairs.

Obtaining Insurance

Trucking businesses need to have insurance coverage to protect against liability and other risks. There are several types of insurance you'll need to consider, including liability insurance, cargo insurance, and physical damage insurance. The cost of insurance can be a significant expense for a trucking business, so it's important to shop around and compare different options to find the best coverage for your business needs.

Setting Up Your Bookkeeping

Good bookkeeping is essential for a successful trucking business. You need to keep accurate records of all your expenses, income, and taxes. This includes keeping track of fuel costs, repairs, and maintenance, as well as invoices and payments from customers. You should consider using accounting software to make bookkeeping easier and more efficient.

Developing Your Marketing Strategy

Marketing is an essential component of any successful business. You need to develop a marketing strategy that targets your ideal customers and sets you apart from the competition. This can include creating a website, social media presence, and advertising in trade publications. It's also important to network and build relationships with other businesses in the industry to increase your visibility and generate more leads.

Hiring the Right Employees

The success of your trucking business relies on the quality of your employees. You need to hire drivers that are qualified, reliable, and have a good safety record. It's also important to hire employees for other roles, such as dispatchers, mechanics, and office staff. When hiring employees, you should conduct thorough background checks and verify their qualifications and references.

Chapter 2

Essential Industry Knowledge

Essential Industry Knowledge: Understanding Trucking Regulations, Logistics, and Freight Management

In the trucking industry, it's essential to have a solid understanding of the regulations, logistics, and freight management that govern the industry. This knowledge is critical to the success of your business and can help you navigate the complex and ever-changing landscape of the trucking industry. In this chapter, we'll explore the essential industry knowledge you need to be a successful trucking business owner.

Trucking Regulations

The trucking industry is heavily regulated by federal and state agencies. To operate a successful trucking business, you need to have a thorough understanding of the regulations that apply to your business. Some of the most important regulations to be aware of include:

- Hours of Service (HOS) regulations: These regulations limit the number of hours a driver can work in a day and week to prevent fatigue and ensure safety.

- Weight and size restrictions: These regulations limit the weight and size of trucks that can travel on certain roads and bridges.

- Electronic Logging Devices (ELDs): ELDs are mandatory devices that record a driver's hours of service to ensure compliance with HOS regulations.

- Drug and alcohol testing: The Federal Motor Carrier Safety Administration (FMCSA) requires all trucking companies to conduct drug and alcohol testing on their employees.

- Commercial Driver's License (CDL) requirements: To operate a commercial vehicle, drivers must have a CDL and meet certain age and driving record requirements.

Logistics

Logistics is the process of planning, implementing, and controlling the movement of goods. In the trucking industry, logistics is critical to ensure that shipments are delivered on time and at the lowest cost possible. Some of the essential logistics knowledge you need to have includes:

- Route planning: Planning the most efficient route for deliveries is critical to minimize costs and ensure timely delivery.

- Load planning: Ensuring that trucks are loaded efficiently and safely is critical to minimize transportation costs and prevent damage to the cargo.

- Freight brokerage: Freight brokers can help you find loads to haul and connect you with shippers and receivers.

- Load tracking: Tracking the location of shipments and providing real-time updates to customers can help build trust and improve customer satisfaction.

Freight Management

Freight management is the process of managing and optimizing the movement of goods to ensure that they're delivered on time and at the lowest cost possible. Some of the essential freight management knowledge you need to have includes:

- Freight pricing: Understanding how to price your freight is critical to remain competitive and profitable.

- Carrier selection: Selecting the right carrier to transport your freight can help reduce costs and ensure timely delivery.

- Freight payment and billing: Managing the payment and billing process for freight is critical to ensure that you get paid on time and accurately.

- Freight tracking and reporting: Tracking the performance of your freight operations and reporting on key metrics can help you identify areas for improvement and optimize your operations.

Conclusion

Having a solid understanding of the regulations, logistics, and freight management that govern the trucking industry is essential to be a successful trucking business owner. By being knowledgeable about the regulations that apply to your business, you can ensure compliance and maintain a good safety record. By understanding logistics and freight management, you can minimize transportation costs, optimize delivery times, and improve customer satisfaction. With this essential industry knowledge, you can build a successful and sustainable trucking business that provides value to your customers and employees.

Chapter 3

The Anatomy of a Truck

The Anatomy of a Truck: Key Components, Maintenance, and Repair

As a trucking business owner, it's essential to have a solid understanding of the anatomy of a truck. Knowing the key components, how to maintain and repair them, and when to replace them can save you time and money in the long run. In this chapter, we'll explore the anatomy of a truck, including the key components, maintenance, and repair.

Key Components of a Truck

A truck is made up of many different components that work together to transport cargo across the country. Some of the key components of a truck include:

- Engine: The engine is the heart of the truck, and it provides the power necessary to haul cargo.

- Transmission: The transmission allows the engine's power to be transmitted to the wheels and enables the driver to shift gears.

- Axles: The axles support the weight of the truck and distribute the weight evenly across the wheels.

- Suspension: The suspension system helps absorb shocks and bumps, providing a smoother ride and reducing wear and tear on the truck.

- Brakes: The brakes are critical for stopping the truck and keeping it under control.

- Tires: The tires are the only part of the truck that makes contact with the road and are essential for ensuring safe and efficient operation.

Maintenance and Repair

Regular maintenance and repair are essential to keep your truck running smoothly and prevent breakdowns on the road. Here are some essential maintenance and repair tasks that you should be aware of:

- Oil changes: Regular oil changes are critical to keep the engine running smoothly and prevent wear and tear.

- Tire maintenance: Regular tire inspections, rotations, and replacements are essential to ensure safe and efficient operation.

- Brake maintenance: Regular brake inspections, replacements, and adjustments are essential for stopping the truck and ensuring safety.

- Electrical system maintenance: Regular inspections and maintenance of the truck's electrical system can prevent breakdowns and ensure that all electrical components are working properly.

- Transmission maintenance: Regular transmission fluid changes and inspections can help prevent damage to the transmission and prolong its lifespan.

- Engine maintenance: Regular engine tune-ups and inspections can prevent breakdowns and extend the life of the engine.

When to Replace Components

Even with regular maintenance and repairs, some components will eventually wear out and need to be replaced. Knowing when to replace these components can help you avoid breakdowns on the road and keep your truck running smoothly. Some of the components that may need to be replaced include:

- Tires: Tires should be replaced when the tread is worn down, or they have become damaged.

- Brakes: Brake pads and shoes should be replaced when they have worn down, or the brakes are not working correctly.

- Engine: Engines may need to be replaced if they become too worn or damaged to be repaired.

- Transmission: Transmissions may need to be replaced if they become too worn or damaged to be repaired.

- Suspension: Suspension components may need to be replaced if they become worn or damaged, causing the truck to ride rough or handle poorly.

Conclusion

Knowing the key components of a truck, how to maintain and repair them, and when to replace them is essential to be a successful trucking business owner. Regular maintenance and repairs can help prevent breakdowns on the road and prolong the life of your truck. By understanding the anatomy of a truck, you can make informed decisions about maintenance, repairs, and replacements, which can save you time and money in the long run. With this knowledge, you can build a successful and sustainable trucking business that provides value to your customers and employees.

Chapter 4

Financing Your Trucking Business

Starting and running a successful trucking business requires a significant amount of capital. You'll need to purchase trucks, hire drivers, cover fuel and maintenance costs, and more. In this chapter, we'll explore strategies for financing your trucking business, including funding options, considerations, and tips to help you secure the capital you need to build and grow your fleet.

Funding Options

There are several options available for financing your trucking business, including:

1. Business Loans: Business loans are a popular option for financing a trucking business. You can apply for a loan through a bank or online lender, and the funds can be used to purchase trucks, equipment, and cover operating costs. Keep in mind that you'll need to have a solid business plan and a good credit score to qualify for a business loan.

2. Equipment Financing: Equipment financing is another option for purchasing trucks and other equipment. With this type of financing, the equipment serves as collateral for the loan, and you make payments over time. This option is often easier to qualify for than a business loan because the equipment is considered less risky collateral.

3. Factoring: Factoring is a type of financing where a third party buys your accounts receivable at a discount, providing you with cash up front. This option can be helpful if you have a lot of outstanding invoices and need cash quickly to cover operating expenses.

4. Leasing: Leasing is an option for obtaining trucks without a large upfront payment. With a lease, you pay a monthly fee to use the truck, and at the end of the lease, you can either purchase the truck or return it to the leasing company.

Considerations

When considering financing options for your trucking business, there are several factors to consider, including:

1. Interest rates and fees: The interest rates and fees associated with loans and financing can vary widely, so it's essential to shop around and compare options to find the best deal.

2. Payment terms: The payment terms of your financing agreement can affect your cash flow and overall financial health. Make sure you understand the terms and can comfortably make the payments before agreeing to a loan or lease.

3. Credit score and history: Your credit score and history will play a significant role in determining your eligibility for financing and the terms you receive.

4. Collateral: Some financing options require collateral, such as equipment or property, which can affect your ability to obtain financing or increase your risk if you default on the loan.

Tips for Securing Financing

Securing financing for your trucking business can be challenging, but there are steps you can take to increase your chances of success. Here are some tips to help you secure the funding you need:

1. Develop a solid business plan: A well-developed business plan can help demonstrate to lenders that you have a clear vision for your business and a plan for success.

2. Improve your credit score: Improving your credit score can increase your chances of securing financing and improve the terms you receive.

3. Be prepared to provide collateral: If you don't have a strong credit history, providing collateral can help you secure financing.

4. Shop around for the best deal: Don't settle for the first financing offer you receive. Shop around and compare options to find the best deal for your business.

5. Consider alternative financing options: Alternative financing options, such as crowdfunding or peer-to-peer lending, may be a good option if traditional financing is not available or desirable.

Conclusion

Financing your trucking business is an essential component of building and growing your fleet. By understanding your options, considerations, and tips for securing financing, you can make informed decisions that support your business goals and objectives. Remember to develop a solid business plan

and improve your credit score, be prepared to provide collateral, shop around for the best deal, and consider alternative financing options. With the right financing strategy, you can secure the funding you need to build and grow a successful trucking business.

In addition to securing financing, it's important to manage your finances carefully to ensure the long-term success of your business. Keep track of your expenses, monitor your cash flow, and establish a budget to help you stay on track. As your business grows, revisit your financing strategy and make adjustments as needed to ensure that you have the capital you need to continue to expand and thrive.

Finally, it's important to work with experienced professionals who can provide guidance and support as you navigate the financing process. Consider working with an accountant or financial advisor who can help you develop a financing strategy and manage your finances effectively. By taking a proactive approach to financing and financial management, you can build and grow a successful trucking business that delivers results for years to come.

Chapter 5

Setting Up Shop

If you're starting a trucking business, there are several important steps you need to take to establish your company and ensure that you're operating legally and safely. In this chapter, we'll cover the essential aspects of setting up shop, including licensing, insurance, and other key considerations.

Business Structure

The first step in setting up your trucking business is to choose a legal structure for your company. This will determine how your business is organized and how you pay taxes. The most common types of legal structures for small businesses are sole proprietorships, partnerships, limited liability companies (LLCs), and corporations. Each structure has its own advantages and disadvantages, so it's important to consult with a business attorney or accountant to determine which option is best for your specific needs.

Licensing

To operate a trucking business legally, you'll need to obtain several different licenses and permits. The specific requirements will vary depending on the state or region in which you plan to operate, but there are some general requirements that apply in most cases.

First, you'll need to obtain a commercial driver's license (CDL) if you plan to drive a truck yourself. This requires passing a written test and a driving test, as well as meeting specific age and medical requirements.

In addition, you'll need to register your business with the Federal Motor Carrier Safety Administration (FMCSA) and obtain a USDOT number. This number is used to track your company's safety record and compliance with federal regulations.

Depending on the type of freight you plan to haul, you may also need to obtain additional permits or licenses. For example, if you plan to transport hazardous materials, you'll need a hazardous materials endorsement on your CDL, as well as additional permits and certifications.

Insurance

One of the most important aspects of setting up your trucking business is obtaining the right insurance coverage. Commercial trucking insurance is essential to protect your company in the event of an accident, theft, or other unexpected events.

The specific types of insurance you'll need will depend on your specific business needs and the types of freight you plan to haul. However, some of the most common types of commercial trucking insurance include:

- Liability insurance: This covers damages and injuries caused by your truck or driver in the event of an accident.

- Physical damage insurance: This covers damage to your truck in the event of an accident or other incident.

- Cargo insurance: This covers the value of the cargo you're transporting in the event of theft, damage, or loss.

- General liability insurance: This covers your business for non-trucking related liabilities, such as slip-and-fall accidents at your business premises.

It's important to work with an experienced insurance agent who can help you determine the types of coverage you need and ensure that you're adequately protected. Don't skimp on insurance to save costs, as it can end up costing you more in the long run.

Other Considerations

In addition to licensing and insurance, there are several other key considerations when setting up your trucking business. These include:

- Equipment: You'll need to invest in a truck or fleet of trucks, as well as other equipment such as trailers and loading docks. Be sure to factor in the cost of maintenance and repairs when budgeting for your business.

- Staffing: If you plan to hire drivers, mechanics, or other employees, you'll need to factor in the cost of salaries, benefits, and other expenses.

- Marketing and advertising: To build a successful trucking business, you'll need to market your services effectively to potential clients. This may include building a website, attending trade shows, or investing in other marketing efforts.

- Compliance: As a trucking company, you'll need to comply with a wide range of federal and state regulations, including hours of service limits, drug testing, and safety inspections. It's important to stay up-to-date with changes to these regulations and ensure that your company is always in compliance.

- Accounting and bookkeeping: As with any business, it's important to keep detailed records of your income and expenses. This will help you stay on top of your finances and ensure that you're making a profit. Consider investing in accounting software or hiring an accountant to help manage your finances.

- Financing: Finally, you'll need to consider how you'll finance your business. Depending on the size of your operation, you may need to secure financing to purchase trucks and other equipment. This can be done through loans or by leasing equipment. Be sure to carefully evaluate your financing options and choose the one that's best for your business.

In conclusion, setting up your trucking business is a complex process that requires careful planning and attention to detail. By following the steps outlined in this chapter, you can establish your business and ensure that you're operating legally and safely. Be sure to work with experienced professionals, such as attorneys, accountants, and insurance agents, to ensure that you're making the right decisions for your business. With the right foundation in place, your trucking business can thrive and grow in the years to come.

Chapter 6

Making the Most of Your Time

One of the keys to success in the trucking industry is efficient route planning and dispatching. By carefully planning your routes and ensuring that your drivers are dispatched to the right locations at the right times, you can improve your efficiency, reduce your costs, and provide better service to your customers.

In this chapter, we'll discuss the strategies and tools you can use to optimize your route planning and dispatching processes. We'll cover the following topics:

- Understanding the importance of route planning and dispatching: Before we dive into the details of how to plan your routes and dispatch your drivers, it's important to understand why these processes are so crucial. By optimizing your routes and dispatching your drivers effectively, you can save time, reduce your fuel costs, and improve your customer service. You'll be able to handle more deliveries with fewer drivers and vehicles, which means you can scale your business without having to invest in more resources.

- Tools for efficient route planning: There are a number of software tools available that can help you plan your routes more efficiently. These tools take into account factors such as traffic patterns, road closures, and delivery schedules to determine the most efficient routes for your drivers. Some of the most popular route planning tools include Route4Me, RoadWarrior, and MyRouteOnline.

- Dispatching your drivers: Once you've planned your routes, you'll need to dispatch your drivers to their assigned locations. This process involves communicating with your drivers, providing them with instructions and updates, and tracking their progress. Many route planning software tools include dispatching features, which can help you automate this process and ensure that your drivers are always on schedule.

- Monitoring and adjusting your routes: Even the most efficient routes can be disrupted by unexpected events, such as traffic jams or accidents. That's why it's important to monitor your routes in real-time and be prepared to make adjustments as needed. You can use GPS tracking systems and other monitoring tools to keep tabs on your drivers and respond quickly to any issues that arise.

- Communication with your customers: Efficient route planning and dispatching can help you improve your customer service by providing more accurate delivery times and reducing the likelihood of missed deliveries. However, it's important to communicate with your customers throughout the process to ensure that they're informed and satisfied. Consider implementing automated tracking and notification systems that provide real-time updates to your customers.

- Best practices for route planning and dispatching: Finally, there are a number of best practices that can help you optimize your route planning and dispatching processes. These include using historical data to inform your planning, avoiding unnecessary stops and detours, and providing your drivers with detailed instructions and maps.

In conclusion, efficient route planning and dispatching are essential components of any successful trucking business. By taking advantage of the tools and strategies discussed in this chapter, you can optimize your routes, reduce your costs, and improve your customer service. Be sure to invest in the right software tools and work closely with your drivers to ensure that you're getting the most out of your resources. With these best practices in place, you'll be well on your way to building a thriving and profitable trucking business.

Chapter 7

Load Boards and Beyond

As a trucking business owner, finding freight and negotiating rates are essential aspects of your operation. Whether you're just starting out or you're looking to grow your business, there are a number of strategies you can use to find freight and build relationships with shippers and brokers.

In this chapter, we'll explore the world of load boards and other tools you can use to find freight, negotiate rates, and build relationships. We'll cover the following topics:

- What are load boards?: Load boards are online marketplaces that connect carriers with shippers and brokers who have freight to move. They provide a platform for carriers to find available loads, negotiate rates, and build relationships with new clients. Some of the most popular load boards include DAT, Truckstop.com, and FreightWaves.

- How to use load boards: To use a load board, you'll typically need to create an account and provide some basic information about your trucking business. Once you're set up, you can search for available loads using criteria such as origin, destination, and type of freight. You can also negotiate rates and communicate with shippers and brokers directly through the load board's messaging system.

- Other strategies for finding freight: In addition to load boards, there are a number of other strategies you can use to find freight. For example, you can reach out to shippers and brokers directly, attend industry events and trade shows, or network with other trucking professionals through online communities and social media.

- Negotiating rates: Negotiating rates is an important part of building a profitable trucking business. When negotiating rates, it's important to understand your costs, including fuel, maintenance, insurance, and driver salaries. You should also be prepared to negotiate based on market conditions and supply and demand for your services.

- Building relationships: Building strong relationships with shippers and brokers can help you secure more consistent and profitable freight. Some strategies for building relationships include providing excellent service, communicating clearly and consistently, and being responsive to your clients' needs. You can also consider offering loyalty discounts or other incentives to encourage repeat business.

- Other tools for building relationships: In addition to load boards, there are a number of other tools you can use to build relationships with shippers and brokers. For example, you can use customer relationship management (CRM) software to keep track of your interactions with clients and automate some of your communications. You can also consider joining industry associations and attending networking events to build your reputation and expand your client base.

In conclusion, finding freight, negotiating rates, and building relationships are all essential components of building a successful trucking business. By taking advantage of load boards and other tools, and by adopting strategies for negotiating rates and building relationships, you can grow your business and increase your profitability. Be sure to stay up-to-date on market conditions and trends in the industry, and always be on the lookout for new opportunities to grow your business. With the right approach, you can establish your trucking business as a trusted and reliable partner in the freight transportation industry.

Chapter 8

Hitting the Road

As a trucking business owner, building a team of reliable and skilled drivers is essential to the success of your business. However, navigating the complex web of regulations governing driver hours-of-service can be challenging. In this chapter, we'll explore the key considerations for building a team of drivers and complying with hours-of-service regulations.

Here are some of the topics we'll cover:

- Recruiting and hiring drivers: Finding and hiring drivers is a key part of building a successful trucking business. When recruiting, consider the qualifications and experience required for the role, as well as factors such as driving record, safety performance, and communication skills. You can also consider offering competitive compensation packages and benefits to attract and retain top talent.

- Training and onboarding drivers: Once you've hired drivers, it's important to provide thorough training and onboarding to ensure they're equipped with the skills and knowledge needed to perform their job safely and effectively. This can include training on driving techniques, safety regulations, and company policies and procedures.

- Managing driver schedules and hours-of-service: Complying with hours-of-service regulations is a critical part of running a trucking business. These regulations govern the maximum amount of time a driver can spend driving and the minimum amount of rest required between driving shifts. To comply with these regulations, you'll need to implement a system for managing driver schedules, including tracking driver hours and ensuring adequate rest periods.

- Choosing the right equipment: Choosing the right equipment is also an important consideration when building a team of drivers. Factors such as the type of freight you'll be hauling, the distance you'll be traveling, and the terrain you'll be navigating should all be taken into account when selecting equipment. You'll also need to consider factors such as fuel efficiency, maintenance costs, and driver comfort when selecting your fleet.

- Ensuring driver safety: Ensuring driver safety is essential to the success of your business. This includes maintaining your vehicles in good working condition, providing regular safety training, and enforcing safety policies and procedures. You can also consider implementing driver safety incentives to encourage safe driving behavior.

- Adapting to changes in the industry: The trucking industry is constantly evolving, and staying up-to-date on industry trends and changes is important for staying competitive. This may include adopting new technologies, such as telematics and electronic logging devices, to improve efficiency and compliance with regulations.

In conclusion, building a team of drivers and complying with hours-of-service regulations are essential aspects of running a successful trucking business. By recruiting and hiring skilled drivers, providing thorough training and onboarding, managing driver schedules and complying with regulations, choosing the right equipment, ensuring driver safety, and adapting to changes in the industry, you can build a thriving trucking business that provides reliable and efficient service to your clients.

Chapter 9

Safety First

Safety is a critical component of any trucking business. Not only is it essential for protecting your drivers and other road users, but it's also important for protecting your business from liability and reputational damage. In this chapter, we'll explore the key considerations for managing risk, training drivers, and protecting your business.

Here are some of the topics we'll cover:

- Managing risk: The first step in ensuring safety is managing risk. This includes identifying potential hazards and implementing measures to mitigate them. Risk management strategies can include vehicle maintenance programs, driver training and safety programs, and insurance policies. It's important to regularly assess and update your risk management strategies to ensure they remain effective.

- Driver training and safety programs: Providing thorough training and safety programs for your drivers is essential to reducing the risk of accidents and ensuring compliance with safety regulations. Driver training can include training on safe driving practices, hazard identification and response, and emergency procedures. You can also implement safety incentives to encourage safe driving behavior.

- Protecting your business: In addition to protecting your drivers and other road users, it's important to protect your business from liability and reputational damage. This can include implementing policies and procedures to ensure compliance with safety regulations, as well as obtaining appropriate insurance coverage. You can also consider partnering with a safety consulting firm to assess and improve your safety program.

- Maintaining your fleet: Proper maintenance of your fleet is another critical component of ensuring safety. Regular maintenance and inspections can help prevent mechanical failures and other safety hazards. You should also establish a vehicle inspection program to ensure that all vehicles are in good working condition and meet safety requirements.

- Responding to accidents: Despite your best efforts to prevent accidents, they can still occur. It's important to have a plan in place for responding to accidents, including procedures for reporting accidents to authorities and insurance companies, providing medical assistance to drivers and other parties involved in the accident, and preserving evidence for investigation.

- Complying with safety regulations: Finally, it's important to ensure that your business is in compliance with all safety regulations. This includes regulations related to driver hours-of-service, vehicle weight and size, and other safety requirements. Failure to comply with safety regulations can result in fines, legal liability, and reputational damage.

In conclusion, safety is an essential component of any trucking business. By managing risk, providing thorough driver training and safety programs, protecting your business, maintaining your fleet, responding to accidents, and complying with safety regulations, you can build a reputation for safety and reliability that sets your business apart from the competition.

Chapter 10

Hauling Hazardous Materials

Hauling hazardous materials is a significant responsibility for any trucking business. Hazardous materials can range from chemicals to flammable liquids, and the risks associated with transporting these materials require extra care and attention. In this chapter, we'll explore the key considerations for compliance, safety, and best practices when hauling hazardous materials.

Here are some of the topics we'll cover:

- Understanding the regulations: The first step in ensuring compliance and safety when hauling hazardous materials is understanding the regulations that apply to your business. Regulations can include the Hazardous Materials Regulations (HMR), which are administered by the Federal Motor Carrier Safety Administration (FMCSA), as well as state-specific regulations. It's important to stay up-to-date on these regulations to ensure compliance and avoid penalties.

- Proper handling and storage: Proper handling and storage of hazardous materials is essential to ensuring safety. This includes using appropriate packaging, labeling, and placarding, as well as securing the materials to prevent shifting or spilling during transport. You should also ensure that your drivers are trained in the proper handling and storage of hazardous materials, and that they understand the risks associated with the materials they are transporting.

- Emergency response: Despite your best efforts to prevent accidents, emergencies can still occur. It's important to have a plan in place for responding to emergencies involving hazardous materials, including procedures for reporting the incident, providing medical assistance to drivers and other parties involved in the incident, and containing and cleaning up spills or releases.

- Safety equipment: In addition to proper handling and storage, it's important to have appropriate safety equipment on board when hauling hazardous materials. This can include fire extinguishers, spill kits, personal protective equipment (PPE), and emergency eyewash stations. It's also important to ensure that your drivers are trained in the use of this equipment.

- Driver training: Thorough driver training is essential to ensuring compliance, safety, and best practices when hauling hazardous materials. Driver training can include training on the proper handling and storage of hazardous materials, as well as emergency response procedures. It's also important to ensure that your drivers are aware of the risks associated with the materials they are transporting.

- Recordkeeping: Proper recordkeeping is essential to ensuring compliance when hauling hazardous materials. This includes maintaining records of training, safety equipment inspections, and emergency response plans. You should also maintain records of any incidents involving hazardous materials and the steps taken to address them.

- Best practices: In addition to complying with regulations and ensuring safety, there are a number of best practices to consider when hauling hazardous materials. This can include avoiding routes that pass through densely populated areas, minimizing stops and delays, and communicating with shippers and receivers to ensure that they are aware of the materials being transported.

In conclusion, hauling hazardous materials requires extra care and attention to ensure compliance, safety, and best practices. By understanding the regulations, properly handling and storing hazardous materials, having an emergency response plan in place, having appropriate safety equipment on board, providing thorough driver training, maintaining proper records, and following best practices, you can ensure the safe and responsible transportation of hazardous materials.

Chapter 11

Managing Your Cash Flow

As the owner of a trucking business, you know that managing your cash flow is essential to keep your business running smoothly. From paying for fuel and maintenance to managing payroll and insurance, cash flow is the lifeblood of your business. In this chapter, we'll explore some strategies for managing your cash flow, including accounting, invoicing, and budgeting.

Accounting for Your Trucking Business

Accounting is the foundation of any successful business, and trucking is no exception. To keep your business running smoothly, you need to have a solid accounting system in place. This will help you keep track of your income and expenses, manage your cash flow, and prepare for tax season.

The first step in setting up your accounting system is to choose the right software. There are many accounting software programs available, and it's important to choose one that is specifically designed for the trucking industry. These programs will include features such as trip sheets, fuel tax reporting, and load tracking.

Once you've chosen your software, it's important to set up your accounts properly. You should have separate accounts for your business and personal expenses, and you should track all of your income and expenses separately. This will make it easier to manage your cash flow and to prepare for tax season.

Invoicing Your Customers

Invoicing is an essential part of running a successful trucking business. You need to ensure that your customers are billed accurately and on time, so that you can receive payment in a timely manner. Late payments can create cash flow problems, so it's important to have a system in place for invoicing your customers.

There are many invoicing software programs available, and you should choose one that is specifically designed for the trucking industry. These programs will allow you to create invoices quickly and easily, and to track payments and outstanding balances.

When invoicing your customers, it's important to include all of the relevant details, such as the date of the delivery, the weight of the shipment, and the rate per mile. You should also include your payment terms, such as the due date and any penalties for late payment.

Budgeting for Growth

Budgeting is an essential part of managing your cash flow and growing your business. A well-planned budget can help you make informed decisions about how to allocate your resources, and can help you identify areas where you can cut costs and increase revenue.

The first step in creating a budget is to identify your fixed costs, such as your lease or mortgage payments, insurance premiums, and equipment maintenance. These costs should be factored into your budget each month.

Next, you should identify your variable costs, such as fuel, repairs, and supplies. These costs will vary from month to month, so it's important to estimate them as accurately as possible.

Finally, you should factor in your revenue, including your expected income from each load. This will give you a clear picture of your cash flow and help you identify areas where you can cut costs and increase revenue.

Conclusion

Managing your cash flow is essential to the success of your trucking business. By setting up a solid accounting system, invoicing your customers accurately and on time, and budgeting for growth, you can keep your business running smoothly and position yourself for long-term success. Remember to track your cash flow regularly and make adjustments as needed to keep your business on track. With careful planning and management, you can grow your trucking business and achieve your goals.

Chapter 12

The Importance of Technology

In today's rapidly evolving world, the importance of technology in the trucking industry can not be understated. It's essential for trucking companies to leverage technology to stay competitive and thrive. One of the most impactful technologies for trucking businesses is telematics and fleet management software. In this chapter, we'll discuss the benefits of these technologies and how they can help streamline your operations.

Telematics is a system that integrates GPS technology, cellular communication, and on-board vehicle sensors to provide real-time data about a vehicle's location, speed, and other performance metrics. Telematics allows trucking companies to monitor and manage their fleets more effectively, resulting in greater efficiency, safety, and profitability.

Fleet management software, on the other hand, provides a comprehensive solution for managing a trucking company's entire fleet of vehicles. This software can track vehicle performance, fuel efficiency, maintenance needs, and other critical data points. It can also manage dispatching, load planning, and driver communication. In combination with telematics, fleet management software can help trucking companies optimize their operations and reduce costs.

The Benefits of Telematics and Fleet Management Software

One of the most significant benefits of telematics and fleet management software is improved safety. By providing real-time data on a vehicle's location and performance, telematics can help trucking companies identify potential safety hazards and take corrective action. For example, if a driver is speeding, a telematics system can send an alert to the driver and the fleet manager, reminding the driver to slow down and comply with safety regulations.

Fleet management software can also improve safety by monitoring driver behavior and identifying patterns that may indicate risky driving practices. This data can be used to coach drivers and implement training programs that promote safe driving habits.

Another benefit of telematics and fleet management software is improved efficiency. By tracking vehicle location and performance, fleet managers can optimize routing, reduce idle time, and eliminate unnecessary miles. This results in reduced fuel costs and increased productivity. In addition, telematics and fleet management software can help trucking companies schedule maintenance and repairs more efficiently, minimizing vehicle downtime and improving overall productivity.

Fleet management software can also help trucking companies reduce paperwork and streamline administrative tasks. By automating tasks such as dispatching, invoicing, and load tracking, companies can reduce errors and improve accuracy. This saves time and reduces the risk of costly mistakes.

Implementing Telematics and Fleet Management Software

Implementing telematics and fleet management software can be a significant investment for a trucking company. However, the benefits of these technologies can far outweigh the costs. To get started, trucking companies should research available solutions and select a provider that meets their specific needs. It's essential to work closely with the provider to ensure a smooth implementation and to train staff on how to use the technology effectively.

Trucking companies should also be prepared to invest in hardware, such as GPS units, and software licenses for all necessary users. The hardware and software should be installed in all vehicles, and drivers should be trained on how to use the technology. Fleet managers should work with drivers to encourage compliance with safety regulations and to promote safe driving habits.

Conclusion

In today's fast-paced business environment, trucking companies must leverage technology to remain competitive. Telematics and fleet management software are powerful tools that can help companies optimize their operations, reduce costs, and improve safety. By implementing these technologies, trucking companies can stay ahead of the competition and continue to grow and succeed.

Chapter 13

Building Your Brand

In today's highly competitive business world, it is crucial for any trucking business to establish a strong brand and differentiate themselves from their competitors. Building a brand can create a unique identity that resonates with customers and sets your business apart in the industry. But how do you go about building your brand in the trucking industry? In this chapter, we will explore the key elements of brand building, from creating a unique brand identity to effective marketing strategies.

Creating a Unique Brand Identity

Before you can start marketing your trucking business, you need to establish a clear and distinct brand identity. A strong brand identity is made up of several key components, including your company name, logo, tagline, and mission statement. Your company name should be memorable and easy to pronounce, while your logo should be visually appealing and easy to recognize. Your tagline should be concise and memorable, conveying your company's unique value proposition. And your mission statement should express your company's core values and goals.

One of the most important elements of a strong brand identity is consistency. All of your marketing materials, from your website to your social media posts, should be consistent in tone, messaging, and design. This consistency creates a sense of trust and familiarity with your customers, which is essential for building a strong brand.

Marketing and Branding Strategies

Once you have established a strong brand identity, the next step is to create effective marketing and branding strategies. In the trucking industry, there are several strategies that can help you promote your business and differentiate yourself from your competitors.

One effective strategy is to focus on a particular niche. By specializing in a specific type of freight or serving a particular geographic area, you can establish a reputation as an expert in your field. This can help you attract customers who value your specialized knowledge and experience.

Another strategy is to leverage social media to promote your brand. By creating engaging content and sharing it on social media platforms like Facebook and LinkedIn, you can build a following and increase brand awareness. Social media can also be a great way to connect with potential customers and build relationships.

Differentiation is also crucial to building a successful brand. By offering unique services or features that your competitors do not, you can set yourself apart in the industry. For example, you might offer 24/7 customer service, or specialize in expedited freight services. Whatever your point of differentiation, make sure it is something that is valuable and meaningful to your target customers.

Measuring Brand Success

As with any business strategy, it is important to measure the success of your branding efforts. One key metric is brand awareness, which measures the percentage of your target audience who are familiar with your brand. You can also measure brand loyalty, which indicates how likely your customers are to choose your business over competitors. Other metrics, such as customer satisfaction and engagement on social media, can also provide valuable insights into the success of your brand.

In conclusion, building a strong brand is essential for success in the trucking industry. By creating a unique brand identity, leveraging effective marketing and branding strategies, and measuring success, you can establish a reputation that sets you apart from your competitors and resonates with your target audience.

Chapter 14

Fostering Strong Relationships with Customers and Shippers

In the trucking industry, building strong relationships with customers and shippers is essential for the success of your business. By providing quality service, you can increase customer satisfaction and loyalty, leading to repeat business and positive word-of-mouth referrals. In this chapter, we'll explore the key elements of fostering strong relationships with customers and shippers.

Understanding Your Customers' Needs

The first step in building strong customer relationships is understanding their needs. By understanding what your customers want and need, you can tailor your services to meet their expectations. Take the time to learn about your customers' businesses, including their products, schedules, and delivery requirements. Ask questions and listen carefully to their answers, and be open to feedback and suggestions for improvement.

Delivering Quality Service

Once you understand your customers' needs, it's time to deliver quality service. This means meeting or exceeding their expectations on every job. Make sure you're delivering shipments on time, communicating effectively, and handling any issues that arise promptly and professionally. By providing quality service, you'll build trust and respect with your customers, leading to long-term relationships.

Communication is Key

Communication is a critical element in building strong relationships with customers and shippers. Be responsive and available to answer any questions or concerns they may have. Keep them informed of any changes to their shipments or delivery schedules, and proactively communicate any potential issues. Make sure your drivers are also trained in effective communication, as they are often the face of your business when interacting with customers.

Respectful and Professional Interactions

Respectful and professional interactions are key to building strong relationships with customers and shippers. Be courteous and respectful in all your interactions, even in difficult situations. Remember that your customers are your partners, and their satisfaction is critical to your success. Treat them with respect, and they will reciprocate by being loyal to your business.

Going the Extra Mile

Going the extra mile can also help build strong relationships with customers and shippers. Consider offering additional services, such as expedited or specialized deliveries, to meet their unique needs. Look for opportunities to add value to their business, such as by providing insights on industry trends or offering cost-saving solutions. By going above and beyond, you'll set your business apart and create loyal customers.

In Conclusion

Building strong relationships with customers and shippers is a critical component of success in the trucking industry. By understanding their needs, delivering quality service, communicating effectively, and demonstrating respect and professionalism, you can create long-term partnerships that will help grow your business. Remember to always put the customer first, and you'll be well on your way to success in the trucking industry.

Chapter 15

Developing a Customer-Centric Culture

In the highly competitive world of trucking, businesses that prioritize the needs of their customers are the ones that thrive. Building a customer-centric culture within your trucking business is key to achieving long-term success. In this chapter, we'll explore the benefits of developing a customer-centric culture and provide practical tips for doing so.

Why a Customer-Centric Culture Matters

The trucking industry is all about moving goods from one place to another, and at the end of the day, the customer is the one who needs those goods delivered. By putting the needs of your customers first, you're not only providing excellent service, but you're also building a loyal customer base. Repeat business is essential to the success of any trucking business, and customers who are happy with the service they receive are more likely to return in the future.

Furthermore, a customer-centric culture can differentiate your business from competitors. In a market where many trucking companies offer similar services, creating a culture that puts customers first can be a powerful way to stand out.

Developing a Customer-Centric Culture

So, how do you go about creating a culture that prioritizes your customers? Here are some key strategies to consider:

1. Set the tone from the top: As the leader of your trucking business, it's up to you to set the tone and make it clear that customer service is a top priority. Make sure that all employees, from drivers to dispatchers to administrative staff, understand the importance of providing excellent service to customers.

2. Hire the right people: Hiring employees who are passionate about providing excellent service is essential. During the hiring process, look for individuals who are naturally empathetic and enjoy helping others. These are the people who are likely to go the extra mile to ensure customer satisfaction.

3. Train your team: Even the most customer-focused employees need training to provide the best service possible. Invest in training programs that teach your team about customer service best practices, as well as the unique needs and challenges of your customers.

4. Listen to your customers: Customer feedback is a valuable tool for improving your service. Encourage your customers to provide feedback, whether through surveys, phone calls, or other means, and make changes based on that feedback.

5. Personalize your service: Customers appreciate when you take the time to understand their unique needs and preferences. When possible, personalize your service to meet those needs. For example, you might assign a driver who is familiar with a particular route or who has experience hauling a particular type of cargo.

6. Communicate effectively: Clear and timely communication is essential to providing excellent service. Make sure that your team communicates regularly with customers, providing updates on the status of their shipments and any changes to their delivery schedules.

By prioritizing customer service, you'll not only build a loyal customer base but also create a culture of excellence within your trucking business. With the right strategies in place, you can differentiate your business from competitors and achieve long-term success in the trucking industry.

Chapter 16

Maintaining Competitive Pricing

In the trucking industry, pricing is a critical factor that can make or break your business. Setting the right prices for your services is important to ensure that your business remains competitive and profitable. To maintain competitive pricing, you need to understand the factors that influence the prices and the strategies that can help you keep your prices competitive. In this chapter, we will discuss the strategies for pricing your freight services and maintaining a competitive edge.

Understand the Market

To set competitive prices, you need to have a good understanding of the market. You should know your competitors, the prices they charge, and the services they offer. You can research the market by using load boards, attending industry events, and networking with other trucking professionals. Once you have a good understanding of the market, you can set your prices based on the value you offer, the quality of your service, and the demand for your services.

Price for Value

Pricing your freight services based on the value you offer is an effective way to differentiate yourself from your competitors. Instead of just offering the lowest prices, you can focus on the value that you offer, such as faster delivery times, better customer service, and specialized equipment. When you price for value, you can charge more for your services because you are offering something unique that your competitors cannot match.

Consider Your Costs

Before you set your prices, it is important to consider your costs. You need to know how much it costs you to operate your business and how much profit you need to make to stay in business. Your costs can include fuel, maintenance, insurance, salaries, and other expenses. Once you know your costs, you can set your prices to cover your expenses and make a profit.

Use a Pricing Strategy

There are several pricing strategies that you can use to maintain competitive pricing. One of the most common strategies is cost-plus pricing, which involves adding a markup to your costs to set your prices. Another strategy is value-based pricing, which involves setting your prices based on the value you offer. You can also use dynamic pricing, which involves adjusting your prices based on supply and demand. By using a pricing strategy, you can set your prices in a way that is consistent with your business goals and the market.

Offer Discounts

Offering discounts is another way to maintain competitive pricing. You can offer discounts for bulk shipments, repeat business, and early payment. Discounts can also be used to attract new customers or to encourage existing customers to use your services more frequently. By offering discounts, you can make your prices more competitive and increase customer loyalty.

Monitor Your Prices

It is important to monitor your prices regularly to ensure that they remain competitive. You should keep track of your competitors' prices and adjust your prices accordingly. You can also use data analytics tools to track your sales and adjust your prices based on customer behavior. By monitoring your prices, you can ensure that you remain competitive and profitable.

Conclusion

Pricing is a critical factor in the success of your trucking business. To maintain competitive pricing, you need to understand the market, price for value, consider your costs, use a pricing strategy, offer discounts, and monitor your prices. By using these strategies, you can set your prices in a way that is consistent with your business goals and the market. Remember that pricing is not just about offering the lowest prices, but about offering value and quality to your customers. By setting the right prices and offering quality service, you can build a strong reputation and attract loyal customers to your business.

Chapter 17

Navigating Competition

In the trucking industry, competition is fierce, and market changes are constant. In order to succeed, it's essential for trucking businesses to be able to navigate these changes, stay ahead of the curve, and grow their business. In this chapter, we'll explore some strategies for doing just that.

1. Keep an Eye on the Market: Staying up-to-date with industry news and trends can help you anticipate market changes before they happen. By regularly monitoring industry publications, attending trade shows and conferences, and participating in industry associations, you can stay informed about what's happening in the industry and identify emerging trends.

2. Be Proactive: When you see changes coming, don't wait for them to impact your business negatively. Instead, take a proactive approach and make changes that position you for success. For example, if you see that demand for certain types of freight is growing, consider investing in equipment that can handle that freight.

3. Diversify Your Services: One way to stay competitive in a constantly changing market is to diversify your services. By offering a range of services, you can appeal to a broader range of customers and protect your business from the impact of market changes. For example, if your business primarily focuses on long-haul trucking, consider offering local delivery services as well.

4. Focus on Quality Service: In a competitive market, quality service can be a key differentiator. By focusing on providing exceptional service to your customers, you can build a loyal customer base that will stick with you even when market conditions are challenging. Make sure your drivers are well-trained, your equipment is well-maintained, and your operations are efficient.

5. Build Strong Relationships: Strong relationships with customers, shippers, and other industry stakeholders can be invaluable in a competitive market. By developing strong relationships with key customers, you can establish a loyal customer base that will help support your business through market changes. Similarly, building strong relationships with shippers and other industry stakeholders can help you stay

informed about market changes and position your business for success.

6. Leverage Technology: Technology can be a powerful tool for staying competitive in the trucking industry. By investing in telematics and fleet management software, you can improve the efficiency of your operations and provide better service to your customers. Additionally, technology can help you stay informed about market changes and identify new opportunities for growth.

7. Stay Flexible: Finally, it's important to remain flexible and adaptable in the face of market changes. By staying nimble and responsive to changing market conditions, you can position your business for success even in challenging times.

Navigating competition in the trucking industry is never easy, but by staying informed, being proactive, diversifying your services, focusing on quality service, building strong relationships, leveraging technology, and remaining flexible, you can position your business for success and grow even in the most challenging of times.

Chapter 18

Growing Your Business

Congratulations, you have successfully built a thriving trucking business! Now, you may be thinking about ways to expand and take your business to the next level. Expanding your fleet and operations can be a daunting task, but with the right strategies and planning, it can be a smooth and successful process.

In this chapter, we will discuss some effective strategies for growing your trucking business and expanding your fleet and operations.

1. Evaluate Your Current Operations

Before you start planning to expand your business, it's important to evaluate your current operations. Take a look at your financials, customer base, and current resources. Analyze your strengths and weaknesses and identify areas that need improvement.

2. Identify Growth Opportunities

Once you've evaluated your current operations, the next step is to identify growth opportunities. Look for new markets or areas where your services are in demand. Consider offering additional services or specialized transportation to set yourself apart from the competition.

3. Plan Your Expansion

Now that you've identified growth opportunities, it's time to plan your expansion. Start by creating a detailed business plan that includes your goals, budget, and timelines. Determine the number of trucks and drivers you'll need and how you'll finance the expansion. You'll also need to consider additional expenses like insurance, permits, and maintenance costs.

4. Recruit and Train Drivers

When expanding your fleet, it's important to recruit and train quality drivers. Look for experienced and reliable drivers who are committed to safety and customer service. Provide them with thorough training to ensure they understand your company's policies and procedures.

5. Utilize Technology

As your business grows, it's essential to utilize technology to streamline operations and improve efficiency. Consider implementing a transportation management system (TMS) or fleet management software to help with dispatching, scheduling, and tracking. These tools can help you optimize routes and reduce costs.

6. Build Strong Relationships

Building strong relationships with customers and shippers is critical for business growth. Delivering quality service and maintaining open communication can help you retain customers and attract new ones. Consider offering incentives or rewards for loyal customers to show your appreciation and build brand loyalty.

7. Monitor and Measure Performance

As you expand your business, it's important to monitor and measure your performance to ensure your goals are being met. Set up a system to track key performance indicators (KPIs) and regularly review your progress. Use this information to make adjustments and fine-tune your operations as needed.

In conclusion, growing your trucking business takes careful planning, hard work, and dedication. Evaluate your current operations, identify growth opportunities, plan your expansion, recruit and train quality drivers, utilize technology, build strong relationships, and monitor and measure performance. By following these strategies, you can successfully expand your fleet and operations and take your business to the next level.

Chapter 19

Specialized Freight Services

As a trucking business owner, you have a wide variety of services that you can offer your customers. While the market is highly competitive, identifying niche markets can help you stand out and grow your business. One way to do this is by offering specialized freight services.

Specialized freight services refer to the transportation of goods that require specific equipment, handling, or expertise. Some examples of specialized freight services include refrigerated transport, oversize and overweight loads, hazmat transportation, and flatbed hauling.

To be successful in specialized freight services, you need to have a solid understanding of the unique requirements of the cargo being transported. You must also have the necessary equipment and specialized knowledge to ensure that the cargo arrives at its destination safely and securely.

One of the most popular specialized freight services is refrigerated transport. This service involves transporting temperature-sensitive cargo, such as food, pharmaceuticals, and medical supplies, in refrigerated trailers. These trailers have temperature control systems that keep the cargo at a specific temperature throughout the journey. It is essential to maintain the temperature within the required range to avoid spoilage, damage, or contamination of the cargo.

Another example of specialized freight services is oversize and overweight loads. This service involves transporting loads that exceed the standard legal limits for weight and size. Oversize and overweight loads require special permits and may need additional equipment, such as pilot cars or police escorts. Additionally, the route must be carefully planned to ensure that it is safe and feasible to transport the load.

Hazmat transportation involves the transportation of hazardous materials that are regulated by the Department of Transportation (DOT). Hazmat transportation requires specialized equipment and training to ensure that the materials are transported safely and comply with DOT regulations. The regulations for hazmat transportation include packaging, labeling, and documentation requirements, as well as specific requirements for handling and transporting the materials.

Flatbed hauling is another specialized freight service that involves the transportation of cargo that cannot be transported in an enclosed trailer. This may include large equipment, machinery, or construction materials. Flatbed trailers are designed to handle oversize, overweight, or irregularly shaped loads. Flatbed hauling requires specialized expertise and equipment to ensure that the cargo is loaded, secured, and transported safely.

To succeed in specialized freight services, you need to understand the unique requirements of the cargo you will be transporting. You should also have the necessary equipment and specialized knowledge to ensure that the cargo arrives at its destination safely and securely. Additionally, you need to have the proper insurance and permits to provide specialized freight services.

Specialized freight services provide opportunities for trucking business owners to differentiate themselves in a highly competitive market. By offering these services, you can tap into niche markets and establish yourself as an expert in a particular area. However, specialized freight services also come with additional risks and costs, such as equipment maintenance, training, and permits. Therefore, it is essential to weigh the benefits and risks carefully before offering specialized freight services.

In summary, specialized freight services offer opportunities for trucking business owners to expand their service offerings and differentiate themselves in a highly competitive market. By understanding the unique requirements of the cargo being transported and having the necessary equipment and specialized knowledge, you can establish yourself as an expert in a particular area. However, it is essential to weigh the benefits and risks carefully before offering specialized freight services to ensure the success and profitability of your business.

Chapter 20

Building a Network

When it comes to growing your trucking business, having a strong network of partners and collaborators can be essential. By building relationships with other businesses in the industry, you can gain access to new customers, increase your efficiency, and open up new opportunities for growth.

Here are some key strategies for building a network of partnerships and collaborations in the trucking industry:

1. Attend Industry Events and Conferences: Industry events and conferences are a great way to meet other trucking business owners, logistics professionals, and industry experts. Look for events that focus on your specific niche or areas of interest, and be sure to take advantage of networking opportunities. Come prepared with business cards, a clear elevator pitch, and questions to ask potential partners.

2. Join Industry Associations: Joining industry associations can be a great way to connect with other businesses in your field. Look for

associations that focus on your niche, and take advantage of the networking events and resources that they offer. Associations can also be a great way to stay up to date on industry news and trends.

3. Partner with Complementary Businesses: Look for businesses that complement your own services and operations, such as freight brokers, dispatch services, or equipment suppliers. Partnering with these businesses can help you to expand your offerings, streamline your operations, and increase your reach.

4. Collaborate with Competitors: While it may seem counterintuitive, collaborating with your competitors can be a great way to grow your business. Look for ways to share resources or partner on larger projects, and be open to opportunities for collaboration that can benefit both parties.

5. Leverage Online Platforms: There are a number of online platforms and marketplaces that can help you to connect with other businesses in the industry. Load boards, freight marketplaces, and logistics platforms can all be great resources for finding new customers and partners. Be sure to research these platforms

thoroughly and choose the ones that are best suited to your business and niche.

6. Build Relationships with Customers and Shippers: Developing strong relationships with your customers and shippers can also help to build your network of partners and collaborators. By delivering quality service and building a reputation for reliability, you can attract repeat business and gain referrals to new customers and partners.

7. Be Open to New Opportunities: Finally, be open to new opportunities for collaboration and partnership. The trucking industry is constantly evolving, and there may be new technologies, services, or business models that can help to expand your operations. By staying open to new ideas and opportunities, you can position your business for long-term success.

Building a strong network of partnerships and collaborations takes time and effort, but the benefits can be significant. By leveraging the expertise, resources, and connections of other businesses in the industry, you can position your trucking business for growth and success in the years to come.

Chapter 21

The Role of Brokers

In the world of trucking, brokers play an important role in connecting carriers with shippers. They act as intermediaries, facilitating transactions between the two parties and helping to ensure that freight is moved from point A to point B as efficiently as possible. But what exactly is a broker, and how can working with one benefit your trucking business?

First, let's define what a broker is. A broker is a person or company that arranges transportation of freight on behalf of shippers. They work with carriers to find available trucks to move the freight, negotiate rates, and handle the paperwork and logistics of the shipment. In return, they receive a commission from the shipper for their services.

There are two types of brokers in the trucking industry: asset-based and non-asset based. Asset-based brokers own and operate their own trucks, while non-asset based brokers do not own any trucks and act solely as intermediaries.

One of the main benefits of working with a broker is the access to a wider pool of shippers and freight.

Brokers often have established relationships with shippers, and can help carriers find new business opportunities. They can also assist carriers in securing loads that may be difficult to find on their own, such as those with specific requirements or for specialized equipment.

Another advantage of working with a broker is the ability to negotiate higher rates for your services. Brokers have experience in negotiating rates with shippers, and can leverage their knowledge of the market to get the best possible rates for carriers. This can help carriers increase their revenue and profitability.

Brokers also handle much of the administrative work associated with shipping, such as billing and invoicing, and can assist carriers with compliance and regulatory issues. This can save carriers time and resources, allowing them to focus on other aspects of their business.

Load boards are another important tool in the trucking industry, and many brokers use them to find available trucks and loads. Load boards are online marketplaces where carriers and shippers can connect and post available freight or trucks. Load boards can be a valuable resource for carriers looking to fill empty trucks, and can help them find loads quickly and efficiently.

However, it's important to note that while brokers and load boards can be valuable resources, they do come with some risks. Some brokers may not pay carriers on time or may fail to disclose all of the details of a load, leading to unexpected costs or delays. It's important for carriers to do their due diligence when working with brokers and load boards, and to establish clear communication and expectations before entering into any agreements.

In summary, brokers and load boards can be valuable resources for carriers looking to expand their business and find new opportunities. They offer access to a wider pool of shippers and freight, can negotiate higher rates, and can handle much of the administrative work associated with shipping. However, it's important for carriers to do their research and establish clear communication and expectations when working with brokers and load boards. With the right approach, brokers and load boards can be powerful tools for carriers looking to grow their business and improve their bottom line.

Chapter 22

Negotiation Tactics

Negotiating rates is a vital part of running a successful trucking business. Whether you are working with shippers or brokers, negotiating the best rates can make a significant impact on your bottom line. However, it's not always an easy task, and it requires preparation, communication, and confidence.

In this chapter, we will discuss negotiation tactics that can help you secure the best rates and maximize your profits.

1. Preparation Preparation is key to any successful negotiation. Before entering into negotiations, you need to have a clear understanding of your costs, including fuel, maintenance, and labor expenses. This knowledge will help you determine your bottom line and make informed decisions during negotiations.

Additionally, you should research the market and the industry trends to get a sense of the going rates. Having this information will give you a solid base

from which to negotiate and will also make it easier
to spot unreasonable offers.

2. Communication Effective communication is
   essential in any negotiation. You need to be
   clear, concise, and confident in presenting your
   rates and explaining your value proposition.
   One useful technique is to ask questions that
   will help you understand the other party's
   needs and objectives.

It's also important to listen actively and be open to
compromise. Try to find a solution that benefits both
parties and keeps the lines of communication open. If
you come across as difficult or confrontational, the
other party may be less willing to work with you in
the future.

3. Negotiation Tactics One common tactic in
   negotiations is to anchor your position with an
   initial offer. This offer should be reasonable and
   based on your preparation and research. From
   this starting point, you can adjust your rates
   and terms based on the other party's response.

Another useful technique is to offer trade-offs that
add value to your services. For example, if a shipper is
looking for faster delivery, you can offer expedited
shipping for a slightly higher rate. This can be a win-

win situation, as the shipper gets the service they need, and you get a higher rate for providing it.

You can also use the "take it or leave it" approach, but this should be reserved for situations where you have significant leverage. This tactic can be risky as it can lead to a stalemate or the other party walking away from the negotiations.

4. Building Relationships Negotiation is not just about getting the best rates; it's also about building strong relationships with your customers and partners. By being fair, transparent, and communicative, you can build trust and goodwill that will lead to long-term partnerships and repeat business.

5. Technology Technology can also be a valuable tool in negotiating rates. Load boards, for example, can provide insights into market rates, enabling you to make informed decisions during negotiations. Additionally, fleet management software can help you optimize your operations and reduce costs, which can make you more competitive in the market.

In conclusion, negotiating rates is an essential skill for any trucking business owner. By preparing, communicating effectively, using tactics, building relationships, and leveraging technology, you can secure the best rates, maximize your profits, and grow your business. Remember that negotiation is not about winning or losing; it's about finding a mutually beneficial solution that works for all parties involved.

Chapter 23

Protecting Your Business

Starting and running a trucking business comes with a number of risks and potential legal pitfalls. While there are many rewards to owning and operating your own business, it is important to be aware of the risks and take steps to protect your company from potential lawsuits, accidents, and other legal issues.

One of the most important things you can do to protect your business is to have a comprehensive insurance policy. You should have insurance coverage for your trucks, cargo, and liability, which will help protect you in the event of an accident or other unforeseen event.

It is also important to maintain strict safety standards and compliance with all relevant regulations. Failure to comply with regulations could result in fines, penalties, or even the loss of your operating license. Stay up to date with the latest regulations and make sure that all of your drivers are properly trained and certified.

Another way to protect your business is to have a solid contract in place for all your customers and vendors. This contract should outline the scope of your services, payment terms, and any other important details. Having a well-written contract can help protect your business in the event of a dispute or legal issue.

In addition to insurance, compliance, and contracts, it is also important to be proactive in managing risk. This includes having a solid safety program in place, performing regular maintenance on your trucks, and staying up to date with the latest technology and safety practices.

When it comes to legal issues, it is important to work with an experienced attorney who specializes in transportation law. This will ensure that you have expert guidance and representation in the event of a legal issue or dispute.

In addition to legal protection, it is also important to have a strong financial management plan in place. This includes managing your cash flow effectively, keeping accurate financial records, and planning for the long-term growth of your business.

Overall, protecting your business involves a combination of insurance, compliance, contracts, risk management, legal representation, and financial management. By taking these steps and staying proactive in managing your business, you can help minimize risks and avoid potential legal pitfalls.

Chapter 24

Expanding Your Offerings

As your trucking business grows, you may start to think about adding new services and diversifying your business. This can help you reach new markets, increase your revenue, and reduce your dependence on a single service. However, expanding your offerings can also be a risky proposition if you don't have a solid plan in place. In this chapter, we'll explore the benefits and challenges of adding new services and provide you with some tips for doing it successfully.

Benefits of Adding New Services

One of the primary benefits of adding new services to your trucking business is the potential for increased revenue. By expanding your offerings, you can tap into new markets and serve a wider range of customers. This can help you build a more diverse customer base, reduce your dependence on a single service, and provide a more stable revenue stream.

Diversification can also help you differentiate your business from competitors. If you're the only trucking company in your area that offers a particular service, you can establish yourself as the go-to provider for that service. This can help you build a reputation as a trusted and reliable provider, which can lead to repeat business and referrals.

Challenges of Adding New Services

Expanding your offerings can also present some challenges. For one, it requires a significant investment of time, money, and resources. You'll need to research the market, identify potential customers, and develop marketing strategies to promote your new services.

Adding new services can also strain your existing resources, particularly if you don't have the staff or equipment to handle the additional workload. You'll need to carefully evaluate your current capabilities and make sure you have the capacity to take on new business without sacrificing the quality of your existing services.

Finally, diversifying your business can be risky if you don't have a solid plan in place. If you're not careful, you could end up spreading yourself too thin or investing in services that don't align with your core competencies. This can lead to financial losses and damage your reputation in the industry.

Tips for Adding New Services

If you're considering adding new services to your trucking business, there are several things you can do to increase your chances of success. Here are some tips to keep in mind:

1. Research the market. Before you invest in a new service, take the time to research the market and identify potential customers. Talk to industry experts, attend trade shows, and conduct online research to gain a better understanding of the market demand and competition.

2. Evaluate your resources. Determine whether you have the staff, equipment, and financial resources to take on new business. If you need to invest in new equipment or hire additional staff, factor these costs into your budget.

3. Develop a marketing plan. Once you've identified a new service to offer, develop a marketing plan to promote it. Identify your target market, create a messaging strategy, and determine which channels to use to reach potential customers.

4. Train your staff. If you're adding a new service, you'll need to train your staff to ensure they have the skills and knowledge to deliver it effectively. This may require additional training or certifications.

5. Monitor your progress. As you roll out new services, keep a close eye on your performance metrics to determine whether you're achieving your goals. Make adjustments as needed to ensure you're delivering the quality of service your customers expect.

In conclusion, expanding your offerings is an important aspect of growing your trucking business. By adding new services and diversifying your operations, you can tap into new markets and increase your revenue streams. However, before jumping into new ventures, it's important to do your research and make sure that the new offerings are feasible and profitable.

You should also consider the impact on your existing operations and make sure that you have the resources and capacity to take on new business. A strong and reliable team, efficient fleet management, and a solid understanding of market demand and competition are essential for success.

Remember, diversification doesn't mean losing focus on your core competencies. It's important to maintain the quality of your core services while adding new offerings. By creating a portfolio of complementary services, you can differentiate yourself from competitors and build a stronger brand.

Expanding your offerings can be a challenging and rewarding process. With careful planning, a customer-centric approach, and a willingness to adapt to changing market conditions, you can successfully grow and diversify your trucking business.

Chapter 25

Fleet Maintenance

Running a successful trucking business means having a reliable fleet of trucks that are well-maintained and in good condition. Proper fleet maintenance is essential for ensuring that your trucks are safe, reliable, and cost-effective to operate. In this chapter, we will explore preventive maintenance and cost reduction strategies that will help you keep your trucks on the road and your business running smoothly.

Preventive Maintenance Preventive maintenance is a proactive approach to maintaining your trucks that involves regularly scheduled maintenance tasks. These tasks are designed to identify and address potential issues before they become major problems. By performing routine maintenance, you can keep your trucks in good condition, avoid breakdowns, and extend the life of your equipment. Here are some key preventive maintenance tasks to consider:

1. Regular Inspections: Inspect your trucks on a regular basis to identify any potential issues. Check the tires, brakes, lights, and other critical

components to ensure that they are working properly.

2. Oil Changes: Regular oil changes are essential for keeping your engine running smoothly. Change the oil according to the manufacturer's recommendations.

3. Fluid Checks: Check your truck's fluids regularly, including brake fluid, transmission fluid, and coolant. Low fluid levels can cause major problems, so it's important to keep them topped off.

4. Filter Replacement: Replace the air and fuel filters regularly to ensure that your engine is getting clean air and fuel.

5. Tire Maintenance: Proper tire maintenance is essential for safety and cost-effectiveness. Check tire pressure, rotate tires regularly, and replace worn tires.

Cost Reduction Strategies In addition to preventive maintenance, there are several cost reduction strategies you can use to keep your fleet operating efficiently. Here are some key strategies to consider:

1. Fuel Management: Fuel costs are a major expense for trucking companies, but there are

ways to reduce your fuel consumption. Consider using fuel-efficient tires, idling reduction technology, and GPS tracking to optimize routes and reduce idle time.

2. Driver Training: Proper driver training can help reduce fuel consumption, prevent accidents, and extend the life of your equipment. Train your drivers to drive defensively, avoid aggressive driving, and perform routine maintenance tasks.

3. Inventory Management: Proper inventory management can help you reduce costs by avoiding overstocking and understocking of parts and supplies. Keep track of your inventory levels and reorder parts as needed.

4. Outsourcing Maintenance: Consider outsourcing some of your maintenance tasks to a third-party service provider. This can help reduce costs and ensure that your trucks are maintained by trained professionals.

5. Technology: Technology can be a powerful tool for reducing costs and improving efficiency. Consider using fleet management software, GPS tracking, and other technologies to optimize your fleet operations.

Conclusion Proper fleet maintenance is essential for running a successful trucking business. By taking a proactive approach to maintenance and using cost reduction strategies, you can keep your trucks on the road, reduce expenses, and increase profitability. Consider implementing these preventive maintenance and cost reduction strategies to keep your business running smoothly.

Chapter 26

Adapting to Market Changes

The trucking industry is constantly evolving, and as a business owner, it's essential to stay on top of emerging trends and adapt your strategies accordingly. By staying informed and taking a proactive approach to change, you can position your business for success in a rapidly evolving marketplace.

Here are some key emerging trends to watch in the trucking industry and strategies for responding to them:

1. Technological Advancements

One of the most significant changes in the trucking industry is the increasing use of technology. From fleet management software to telematics, technology is driving efficiency, improving safety, and enhancing the overall customer experience.

To adapt to this trend, consider investing in technology that can help you manage your fleet more effectively. This may include tools for tracking fuel consumption, optimizing routes, and monitoring driver performance. By embracing technology, you can streamline operations, reduce costs, and stay competitive in an increasingly tech-driven industry.

2. Environmental Sustainability

As concerns about climate change continue to grow, there is increasing pressure on businesses to reduce their carbon footprint. This is particularly true in the trucking industry, which accounts for a significant portion of greenhouse gas emissions.

To respond to this trend, consider investing in eco-friendly equipment and practices, such as hybrid or electric trucks, aerodynamic designs, and fuel-efficient engines. By demonstrating a commitment to sustainability, you can attract environmentally conscious customers and differentiate your business from competitors.

3. E-commerce Growth

The rise of e-commerce has dramatically impacted the trucking industry. With the explosion of online shopping, there is increasing demand for last-mile delivery services, which require a fleet of smaller, more agile vehicles.

To adapt to this trend, consider expanding your offerings to include last-mile delivery services. This may require investing in a new fleet of smaller vehicles, hiring additional drivers, and partnering with e-commerce retailers. By diversifying your business and offering a wider range of services, you can capitalize on this growing market and stay ahead of the competition.

4. Driver Shortage

The trucking industry is facing a significant driver shortage, which is expected to worsen in the coming years. With many older drivers retiring and younger generations showing little interest in the profession, finding and retaining qualified drivers has become a major challenge for businesses.

To respond to this trend, consider offering competitive wages and benefits packages to attract and retain top talent. You may also want to invest in training and development programs to help your drivers improve their skills and advance their careers. By focusing on employee satisfaction and investing in your workforce, you can build a strong and stable team that can help your business thrive.

5. Changing Regulations

The trucking industry is highly regulated, and changes to regulations can have a significant impact on businesses. For example, recent changes to hours-of-service regulations have placed greater restrictions on driver work hours, which can impact delivery times and productivity.

To adapt to changing regulations, it's essential to stay informed and up-to-date on the latest developments. You may also want to work with a regulatory compliance specialist to ensure that your business is in full compliance with all relevant regulations. By taking a proactive approach to compliance, you can avoid legal pitfalls and maintain the trust of your customers.

Conclusion

Adapting to emerging trends is essential for any business that wants to thrive in a rapidly changing marketplace. By staying informed and taking a proactive approach to change, you can position your business for success in the trucking industry. Whether you're investing in technology, expanding your offerings, or improving driver retention, there are many strategies you can use to stay ahead of the competition and build a thriving business.

Chapter 27

Implementing Environmental and Sustainability Practices

In recent years, there has been a growing focus on environmental and sustainability practices in the trucking industry. As a trucking business owner, it's important to consider how your operations can reduce your carbon footprint, minimize your environmental impact, and promote sustainability.

Implementing environmental and sustainability practices in your trucking business not only benefits the environment, but it can also have economic benefits, such as cost savings and increased customer loyalty. Here are some strategies for reducing your carbon footprint and promoting sustainability in your trucking operations:

1. Invest in Fuel-Efficient Vehicles: Consider investing in fuel-efficient vehicles that meet the latest emissions standards. While these vehicles may have a higher upfront cost, they can save you money in the long run by reducing fuel consumption and maintenance costs.

2. Adopt Green Driving Practices: Encourage your drivers to adopt green driving practices, such as reducing idling time, avoiding hard braking and acceleration, and maintaining a steady speed. These practices not only reduce fuel consumption but also improve safety.

3. Utilize Alternative Fuels: Consider utilizing alternative fuels, such as biodiesel, compressed natural gas, or electric, in your fleet. These fuels can reduce emissions and provide cost savings over time.

4. Efficient Route Planning: Plan routes that are the most efficient in terms of distance and time. This reduces fuel consumption and emissions, while also saving time and money.

5. Load Consolidation: Consolidate shipments to reduce the number of trips needed and minimize the amount of fuel and resources required.

6. Use Telematics and Fleet Management Software: Implement telematics and fleet management software to monitor fuel consumption, driver behavior, and vehicle performance. These tools can help you identify

areas for improvement and optimize your operations.

7. Recycling and Waste Reduction: Implement recycling and waste reduction programs in your offices and warehouses. This not only helps the environment, but can also save you money on waste disposal fees.

8. Partner with Eco-Friendly Companies: Consider partnering with other companies that share your commitment to sustainability. This can help you reduce your environmental impact and strengthen your brand.

9. Stay Up-to-Date on Regulations: Stay up-to-date on the latest environmental and sustainability regulations and compliance requirements. This will help you avoid penalties and fines and demonstrate your commitment to sustainability.

By implementing these strategies, you can reduce your carbon footprint and promote sustainability in your trucking business. This not only benefits the environment, but can also improve your bottom line and enhance your reputation in the industry.

Chapter 28

Industry Advocacy

The trucking industry is constantly evolving, and it's important to stay up-to-date with the latest developments and advocacy efforts that can impact your business. From regulatory changes to technological advances, there are many factors that can affect the trucking industry, and it's crucial to stay informed to protect your interests.

In this chapter, we'll explore the importance of staying current with industry developments and participating in advocacy efforts, as well as some of the key ways to get involved.

Why Industry Advocacy Matters

The trucking industry is heavily regulated, and changes to laws and regulations can have a significant impact on businesses. For example, new emissions standards, hours-of-service regulations, and other changes can increase costs, reduce productivity, and create other challenges for trucking companies.

Industry advocacy is the process of advocating for the interests of the trucking industry with government officials and other stakeholders. By staying informed and participating in advocacy efforts, trucking companies can help shape the policies and regulations that affect their businesses.

In addition to the potential economic benefits, industry advocacy can also help promote safety, sustainability, and other values that are important to the industry. By working together to promote best practices and common standards, the industry can help improve its image and reputation with customers, regulators, and the public.

Getting Involved in Industry Advocacy

There are many ways to get involved in industry advocacy, and it's important to find the methods that work best for your business. Here are a few key options to consider:

1. Join Industry Associations: Industry associations, such as the American Trucking Associations (ATA) and the Owner-Operator Independent Drivers Association (OOIDA), provide a platform for trucking companies to come together and advocate for their interests. By joining an association, you can stay informed

about industry developments and participate in advocacy efforts at the local, state, and national levels.

2. Attend Industry Events: Industry events, such as conferences and trade shows, provide opportunities to connect with other industry professionals and learn about the latest trends and developments. By attending these events, you can stay informed about industry changes and network with other trucking companies and industry stakeholders.

3. Engage with Legislators: Legislators at the local, state, and national levels play a key role in shaping the policies and regulations that affect the trucking industry. By reaching out to your representatives and engaging with them on industry issues, you can help ensure that your interests are represented in the policymaking process.

4. Participate in Advocacy Campaigns: Industry associations and other organizations often lead advocacy campaigns to promote specific policy positions or to oppose harmful regulations. By participating in these campaigns, you can help amplify your voice and make a difference on key industry issues.

5. Stay Informed: Staying informed about the latest developments in the industry is crucial for effective advocacy. By reading industry publications, attending webinars, and participating in other educational opportunities, you can stay up-to-date on the latest industry trends and issues.

Conclusion

The trucking industry is a complex and dynamic field, and staying informed about the latest developments and participating in advocacy efforts is crucial for success. By working together to promote common standards, advocate for industry interests, and promote best practices, the trucking industry can help improve its reputation and create a more sustainable future. Whether through joining an industry association, attending industry events, engaging with legislators, or participating in advocacy campaigns, there are many ways to get involved and make a difference in the industry.

Chapter 29

Staying Ahead of the Curve

In today's fast-paced world, staying ahead of the curve is crucial for the success of any business, including those in the trucking industry. As technology continues to evolve and disrupt traditional business models, it's essential to stay up-to-date and embrace new developments to remain competitive and relevant. In this chapter, we'll explore how you can stay ahead of the curve by embracing disruptive technologies and trends.

1. Embrace Technology

One of the most significant disruptions in the trucking industry is technology. Fleet management software, telematics, and GPS tracking have transformed the way trucking businesses operate, making them more efficient, cost-effective, and environmentally friendly.

To stay ahead of the curve, it's crucial to embrace these technologies and make them an integral part of your business. Implementing fleet management software can help you monitor your fleet's performance, track fuel consumption, and optimize routes, leading to cost savings and increased productivity.

Telematics systems can also help you keep track of your trucks' location and monitor driver behavior, which can improve safety and reduce fuel costs. Additionally, GPS tracking can help you stay on top of deliveries, ensuring that your customers receive their goods on time.

2. Keep Up with Industry Trends

Another way to stay ahead of the curve is to keep up with emerging trends in the industry. This could include changes in regulations, market trends, and new technologies.

For instance, as electric vehicles become more prevalent, it may be worth considering how this technology could fit into your business. Additionally, the rise of e-commerce has led to an increase in last-mile delivery services, creating new opportunities for trucking businesses.

By staying up-to-date with industry developments, you can identify new opportunities for growth and adjust your business strategy accordingly.

3. Be Agile

One of the hallmarks of successful businesses is their ability to adapt quickly to changes in the market. To stay ahead of the curve, it's essential to be agile and flexible in your approach.

This could mean being open to new business models, such as partnering with other businesses, or being willing to experiment with new technologies.

4. Embrace Sustainability

Sustainability is another critical trend in the trucking industry. With the growing concern about climate change, many businesses are looking for ways to reduce their carbon footprint and operate more sustainably.

By embracing sustainability, you can reduce your operating costs and attract customers who are looking for eco-friendly solutions. This could include investing in alternative fuels or hybrid vehicles, improving your supply chain management, and reducing waste.

5. Participate in Industry Advocacy

Finally, it's essential to participate in industry advocacy efforts. By staying informed about industry developments and engaging with policymakers, you can help shape the future of the trucking industry.

This could include supporting policies that promote safety, sustainability, and innovation or participating in industry groups that advocate for the interests of trucking businesses.

Conclusion

In conclusion, staying ahead of the curve in the trucking industry requires a willingness to embrace disruptive technologies and emerging trends, as well as being agile and flexible in your approach. By keeping up with industry developments, embracing sustainability, and participating in industry advocacy efforts, you can position your business for success in a rapidly changing industry.

Chapter 30

Addressing the Driver Shortage

As the trucking industry continues to grow and evolve, one of the biggest challenges that companies face is the ongoing shortage of qualified drivers. With an aging workforce and increasing demand for freight transportation, it's more important than ever to prioritize driver recruitment, retention, and positive work culture. In this chapter, we'll discuss some strategies for addressing the driver shortage and building a strong team of drivers for your business.

Recruitment One of the first steps in addressing the driver shortage is to focus on recruitment efforts. This means actively seeking out new drivers through various channels, such as job postings, referrals, and networking. Some strategies to consider include:

1. Creating a positive brand image: A company's reputation and brand image can play a big role in attracting new drivers. By creating a positive work culture and offering competitive benefits and compensation, companies can increase their appeal to potential drivers.

2. Partnering with driver training schools:
   Partnering with local truck driving schools can
   provide a valuable source of new drivers who
   are already trained and licensed.

3. Attending job fairs and industry events:
   Attending job fairs and industry events can give
   companies the opportunity to connect with
   potential drivers in person and share
   information about their company and available
   positions.

Retention Once you have recruited new drivers, the
next step is to focus on retention. Driver retention
can be challenging in the trucking industry, where
long hours, time away from home, and high-stress
environments can lead to burnout and turnover.
However, by focusing on driver satisfaction and work-
life balance, companies can create a positive work
culture that encourages drivers to stay with the
company for the long term. Some strategies to
consider include:

1. Offering competitive pay and benefits:
   Competitive compensation and benefits
   packages can help to attract and retain drivers.

2. Providing opportunities for professional
   development and advancement: Providing

training and opportunities for advancement can help to keep drivers engaged and motivated.

3. Fostering a positive work environment: Creating a positive work environment, including open communication, regular feedback, and recognition for good performance, can help to build a strong sense of team and community among drivers.

Work Culture In addition to recruitment and retention efforts, it's important for companies to focus on creating a positive work culture that prioritizes driver satisfaction and well-being. This means not only providing competitive pay and benefits, but also focusing on aspects of the job that can impact driver quality of life, such as work-life balance, safety, and mental health. Some strategies to consider include:

1. Prioritizing safety: Creating a culture of safety, including regular safety training and communication, can help to reduce accidents and promote driver well-being.

2. Offering flexible scheduling: Offering flexible scheduling, such as home time options and predictable routes, can help drivers to balance work and personal life.

3. Providing mental health support: The trucking industry can be a high-stress environment, and companies can support driver well-being by providing resources and support for mental health and wellness.

Conclusion Addressing the driver shortage is one of the biggest challenges facing the trucking industry today. By focusing on recruitment, retention, and positive work culture, companies can build strong teams of drivers that are equipped to meet the demands of the industry. As the industry continues to evolve, it's important for companies to remain flexible and responsive to the changing needs and expectations of drivers, and to prioritize their well-being and satisfaction as key drivers of business success.

Chapter 31

Staying Safe on the Road

As a trucking company, one of your top priorities should be ensuring the safety of your drivers and assets while on the road. Not only is it important for the well-being of your team, but it is also crucial for maintaining the reputation and success of your business. In this chapter, we will explore various strategies for staying safe on the road, including driver training, vehicle maintenance, and safety protocols.

Driver Training

One of the most effective ways to keep your drivers safe on the road is by providing them with comprehensive training. This training should cover various aspects of safe driving, including defensive driving techniques, hazard recognition, and proper vehicle handling. By investing in quality training, you can help your drivers develop the skills and knowledge necessary to prevent accidents and navigate dangerous situations.

In addition to general safe driving practices, it is also important to provide your drivers with specialized training for unique circumstances. For example, if your company hauls hazardous materials, your drivers should receive training on the specific regulations and safety protocols for transporting those materials. By providing your drivers with the knowledge and skills necessary to handle any situation, you can help prevent accidents and keep them safe on the road.

Vehicle Maintenance

Another crucial aspect of staying safe on the road is proper vehicle maintenance. Regular maintenance can help identify potential issues before they become serious problems, reducing the likelihood of breakdowns and accidents. It is important to establish a maintenance schedule and ensure that all vehicles are inspected and serviced according to that schedule.

In addition to routine maintenance, it is also important to conduct pre-trip inspections. Before each trip, drivers should inspect their vehicles thoroughly to ensure that all components are functioning properly. This includes checking brakes, lights, tires, and other critical systems. By conducting thorough inspections, drivers can identify any issues and address them before they become safety hazards.

Safety Protocols

In addition to driver training and vehicle maintenance, it is also important to establish and enforce safety protocols. These protocols should cover a range of topics, including accident response procedures, driver behavior expectations, and compliance with hours-of-service regulations.

For example, your company should have clear guidelines for how drivers should respond in the event of an accident. This may include reporting the incident to a supervisor, documenting any damages or injuries, and providing assistance to any other parties involved. By establishing clear protocols, you can ensure that your drivers are prepared to handle accidents in a safe and efficient manner.

Similarly, you should have expectations for driver behavior, including rules for distracted driving, drug and alcohol use, and proper use of safety equipment. By setting clear expectations and enforcing them consistently, you can help prevent unsafe behavior and keep your drivers safe on the road.

Finally, it is crucial to ensure that your drivers are compliant with hours-of-service regulations. These regulations are designed to prevent driver fatigue, which is a major cause of accidents in the trucking industry. By establishing and enforcing strict compliance with these regulations, you can help prevent accidents and keep your drivers safe.

Conclusion

Staying safe on the road is essential for the success of your trucking company. By investing in driver training, vehicle maintenance, and safety protocols, you can reduce the likelihood of accidents and protect your drivers and assets. By establishing a culture of safety within your company, you can also help maintain your reputation and ensure the continued success of your business.

Chapter 32

Handling Challenges

In the trucking industry, challenges can arise at any time, from delays and missed appointments to mechanical issues and weather-related obstacles. Being able to handle these challenges effectively is essential for maintaining a successful business. This chapter will discuss some common issues that arise in the industry and provide strategies for addressing them.

Dealing with customers and shippers

Customer service is a critical part of any business, and the trucking industry is no exception. When dealing with customers and shippers, it's essential to be professional and polite at all times. However, sometimes, conflicts can arise, and it's important to have strategies in place for addressing them.

One of the most common customer-related issues is a late or missed delivery. In this situation, it's essential to communicate with the customer as soon as possible to let them know what has happened and what steps are being taken to rectify the situation. Apologizing for the inconvenience and offering a solution can go a long way in maintaining a positive relationship with the customer.

Another issue that can arise is damage to the cargo during transport. In this situation, it's crucial to document the damage and report it to the customer as soon as possible. Taking photos and providing detailed reports can help to minimize any disputes and ensure that any necessary compensation is paid.

Sometimes, issues can also arise with the shipper. For example, a shipper may provide incorrect or incomplete information, resulting in delays or missed appointments. In these situations, it's important to communicate clearly with the shipper and make sure that all necessary information is provided before departing.

Handling employee issues

In addition to customer and shipper issues, it's also essential to be prepared to handle employee-related challenges. Employee issues can range from interpersonal conflicts to issues related to performance and productivity.

When it comes to interpersonal conflicts, it's important to address the issue as soon as possible. Encouraging open communication and working to find a solution that is satisfactory for all parties involved can help to prevent conflicts from escalating.

In situations where an employee is not meeting expectations related to performance or productivity, it's important to have a plan in place for addressing the issue. This might involve providing additional training or support, setting clear expectations and goals, and monitoring progress over time.

Dealing with unexpected challenges

While it's important to be prepared for common issues that arise in the industry, unexpected challenges can also arise. For example, weather-related events or mechanical issues can cause significant disruptions to operations.

In these situations, communication is key. Making sure that all stakeholders are informed of the situation and providing regular updates can help to minimize the impact of the disruption. It's also important to have contingency plans in place for handling unexpected events.

Conclusion

In the trucking industry, challenges can arise at any time, from customer-related issues to employee conflicts and unexpected events. Being prepared to address these challenges effectively is essential for maintaining a successful business. By focusing on customer service, communication, and contingency planning, it's possible to handle even the most challenging situations in a professional and effective manner.

Chapter 33

The Importance of Communication

In the trucking industry, communication is key. From dispatchers to drivers, to customers and shippers, effective communication can make or break a business. Building a culture of open communication can improve operational efficiency, prevent misunderstandings, and ultimately drive success. In this chapter, we will explore the importance of communication in the trucking industry and provide strategies for building effective communication channels in your business.

Why Communication is Crucial in the Trucking Industry

In the trucking industry, there are a variety of stakeholders involved in the transportation process. Dispatchers need to communicate with drivers to ensure they are on track to deliver the shipment on time. Drivers need to communicate with dispatchers if they encounter unexpected roadblocks or other issues that may impact the delivery schedule. Customers and shippers need to communicate with carriers to ensure that their needs are being met and that the delivery process is running smoothly.

Effective communication can improve operational efficiency in a number of ways. It can ensure that drivers are on the most efficient route, that they are aware of any changes to the delivery schedule, and that they are able to address any issues as they arise. Open communication can also help build stronger relationships with customers and shippers, leading to more repeat business and referrals.

Building Effective Communication Channels

To build effective communication channels in your business, it is important to establish a culture of open communication. This means setting expectations for how communication should take place and encouraging all stakeholders to participate.

One way to build a culture of open communication is to hold regular meetings with all stakeholders involved in the transportation process. This may include dispatchers, drivers, customers, and shippers. During these meetings, everyone can share updates and discuss any issues that may have arisen. This can help ensure that everyone is on the same page and can proactively address any problems before they become more significant.

Another strategy for building effective communication channels is to implement technology that streamlines the communication process. This may include a mobile app that allows drivers to easily communicate with dispatchers or software that provides real-time updates on shipment status. By providing drivers and other stakeholders with the tools they need to communicate effectively, you can help ensure that everyone is informed and up-to-date on the latest developments.

It is also important to provide training on effective communication techniques for all stakeholders involved in the transportation process. This can include training on active listening, conflict resolution, and effective writing skills. By providing your employees with the tools they need to communicate effectively, you can help prevent misunderstandings and ensure that everyone is on the same page.

The Role of Leadership in Communication

Leadership plays a critical role in building effective communication channels in a business. Leaders should set the tone for communication by modeling open and transparent communication themselves. They should encourage employees to ask questions and provide feedback and be responsive to concerns raised by all stakeholders.

Leaders should also be willing to listen to feedback and use it to improve communication processes within the business. This may involve adjusting processes, implementing new technology, or providing additional training to employees.

Finally, leaders should encourage a culture of continuous improvement when it comes to communication. This means that they should always be looking for ways to improve communication channels and processes within the business. By prioritizing effective communication, leaders can help drive operational efficiency and improve relationships with customers and shippers.

Conclusion

Effective communication is crucial in the trucking industry. By building effective communication channels, you can improve operational efficiency, prevent misunderstandings, and drive success. To do so, it is important to establish a culture of open communication, implement technology that streamlines the communication process, and provide training on effective communication techniques. Leadership plays a critical role in this process by modeling open and transparent communication, being responsive to feedback, and encouraging a culture of continuous improvement. By prioritizing effective communication, you can help ensure that your business is successful

Chapter 34

Building a Resilient Business

In the trucking industry, success isn't just about working hard and delivering loads on time. It's also about being prepared for the unexpected. Economic downturns, market changes, and other disruptions can have a significant impact on your business. Therefore, it's essential to build a resilient business that can weather any storm.

So, how can you prepare your business for economic downturns and market changes? Here are some strategies to help you stay resilient.

1. Diversify your services and customers

One of the best ways to prepare for market changes is to diversify your services and customers. By offering a variety of services, you can be more adaptable to changing market demands. Additionally, by working with different customers, you can reduce your dependence on any one customer or industry.

For example, if you primarily transport goods for the automotive industry, consider expanding your services to include other industries such as healthcare or retail. Similarly, if you only work with large companies, consider working with smaller businesses as well.

2. Maintain a healthy cash flow

Maintaining a healthy cash flow is critical for any business, especially during tough economic times. Make sure to keep track of your expenses, invoices, and payments. Avoid late payments, as they can negatively impact your cash flow.

Consider using accounting software to help manage your finances, and have a plan for how you'll handle unexpected expenses. Keep a financial buffer to help you stay afloat in times of economic hardship.

3. Focus on efficiency and cost reduction

Efficiency and cost reduction can help your business stay profitable during economic downturns. Look for ways to streamline your operations, reduce waste, and cut costs without sacrificing quality.

For example, consider implementing a preventive maintenance program to keep your fleet in good condition, reducing the risk of expensive breakdowns. Additionally, make sure your drivers are following safe driving practices to reduce the risk of accidents and the associated costs.

4. Keep an eye on market trends

Staying up-to-date on market trends can help you identify potential threats or opportunities. Keep an eye on economic indicators such as GDP and inflation, as well as industry-specific trends.

By staying informed, you can make more informed decisions about your business. For example, if you notice that demand for a particular service is decreasing, you can adjust your offerings accordingly.

5. Build strong relationships with customers and suppliers

Building strong relationships with your customers and suppliers can help you weather economic downturns. By maintaining good relationships with your customers, you're more likely to retain their business even during tough times. Similarly, by working closely with your suppliers, you can negotiate better prices and more favorable terms.

Additionally, consider forming partnerships with other businesses in your industry. By collaborating with other companies, you can share resources and knowledge, which can be especially valuable during challenging times.

6. Plan for the future

Finally, it's important to plan for the future. Think about where you want your business to be in five, ten, or twenty years. Consider how changes in the industry or economy might impact your business, and have a plan in place to address these challenges.

Additionally, make sure to regularly review and update your business plan to ensure it reflects your current goals and situation.

In conclusion, building a resilient business is essential for success in the trucking industry. By diversifying your services and customers, maintaining a healthy cash flow, focusing on efficiency and cost reduction, staying informed about market trends, building strong relationships with customers and suppliers, and planning for the future, you can prepare your business for economic downturns and market changes. Remember, being proactive and prepared is key to staying ahead of the curve in the trucking industry.

Chapter 35

Managing Your Reputation

In today's digital age, online reputation management has become increasingly important for businesses in all industries, including the trucking industry. Your online reputation can make or break your business, and it's essential to have a positive image and reputation that reflects your values, mission, and services.

In this chapter, we'll discuss the importance of online branding and reputation management strategies, and how trucking businesses can build and maintain a strong online presence.

The Importance of Online Branding

Online branding is a crucial element of any business, and it's especially important for trucking companies. Your online brand is what sets you apart from your competitors and defines your company's personality, values, and mission. By building a strong online brand, you can create an emotional connection with your audience and stand out in a crowded market.

Your online brand is more than just a logo and a website. It includes everything from your social media profiles to your customer reviews, and everything in between. The goal is to create a consistent and cohesive brand message across all channels, which will help you build a loyal following and drive more business.

Building Your Online Presence

One of the first steps in building your online reputation is to establish a strong online presence. This means creating a website that accurately represents your business, as well as social media profiles on platforms like Facebook, Twitter, and LinkedIn.

Your website should be easy to navigate, visually appealing, and contain all the necessary information about your business, including your services, location, and contact information. It's also essential to ensure that your website is optimized for search engines, which will help you rank higher in search results and attract more visitors to your site.

Social media is also an essential part of your online branding strategy. By creating social media profiles and posting regular updates, you can engage with your audience, share your expertise, and build your online reputation. It's important to choose the right social media platforms that make sense for your business and target audience.

Managing Your Online Reputation

Once you have established your online presence, it's essential to manage your online reputation. This means monitoring what people are saying about your business online and taking steps to address any negative reviews or comments.

There are several tools and services available to help you manage your online reputation, including social media monitoring tools and online reputation management services. These services can help you track what people are saying about your business online, respond to negative reviews or comments, and proactively build a positive online reputation.

One of the most effective ways to manage your online reputation is by encouraging your customers to leave positive reviews. Positive reviews can help build trust and credibility, and they can also improve your search engine rankings. You can encourage your customers to leave reviews by including links to your review profiles on your website, social media profiles, and email signature.

Handling Negative Reviews

Negative reviews are an inevitable part of doing business, but how you handle them can make a big difference in your online reputation. When responding to negative reviews, it's essential to remain professional and courteous, even if you disagree with the reviewer's comments.

It's important to address the issue and offer a solution or explanation for the problem. This shows that you are proactive about addressing customer concerns and are committed to providing excellent customer service.

If the negative review is untrue or malicious, it may be appropriate to report it to the platform where it was posted. Most review sites have policies in place to address false or malicious reviews, and they will investigate and remove them if necessary.

Conclusion

In conclusion, online branding and reputation management are essential for trucking businesses that want to build a positive image and reputation. By establishing a strong online presence, monitoring what people are saying about your business online, and taking proactive steps to address any negative comments, you can build a loyal following and drive more business.

Chapter 36

Taking Care of Yourself

n the fast-paced world of transportation and logistics, it's easy to get caught up in the day-to-day challenges of running a business. But amidst the hustle and bustle, it's important not to forget about one of the most important aspects of any successful endeavor: taking care of yourself. In this chapter, we'll explore some strategies for managing your work-life balance and personal well-being, so you can be at your best both in and out of the workplace.

One of the biggest challenges facing many business owners and entrepreneurs is finding a healthy balance between work and personal life. It's easy to get caught up in the never-ending cycle of tasks and responsibilities, but it's important to remember that taking care of your own well-being is just as important as taking care of your business.

One way to start finding that balance is to set clear boundaries between work and personal time. Make a schedule that outlines when you'll be working and when you'll be taking time for yourself, and stick to it as much as possible. If you have a tendency to check emails or take work calls outside of work hours, try setting specific times when you'll be available for those tasks, and avoid doing them outside of those designated times.

Another important aspect of maintaining a healthy work-life balance is making time for self-care. This can look different for everyone, but it's important to prioritize activities that help you unwind and recharge, whether that's exercise, meditation, spending time with loved ones, or pursuing hobbies and interests outside of work.

In addition to finding a healthy balance between work and personal life, it's also important to prioritize your own physical and mental health. This includes getting enough sleep, eating a balanced diet, and staying physically active. It's also important to take care of your mental health by managing stress, seeking support when needed, and taking time for relaxation and self-reflection.

As a business owner or entrepreneur, it can be easy to put your own needs and well-being on the backburner in order to focus on the needs of your business. But the truth is, taking care of yourself is an essential part of building and maintaining a successful enterprise. By finding a healthy work-life balance, prioritizing self-care, and taking steps to maintain your physical and mental health, you'll be better equipped to handle the challenges and stresses of running a business.

It's also important to remember that taking care of yourself doesn't just benefit you personally—it can also benefit your business. By prioritizing your own well-being, you'll be more productive, more focused, and better equipped to handle the challenges that come your way. You'll also set a positive example for your employees, demonstrating the importance of work-life balance and self-care.

In conclusion, taking care of yourself is an essential part of building and maintaining a successful business. By prioritizing your own well-being, you'll be better equipped to handle the challenges of running a business, and you'll set a positive example for your employees. So don't forget to make time for self-care, and remember that taking care of yourself is just as important as taking care of your business.

Chapter 37

The Future of Trucking

The trucking industry is a critical component of the global supply chain, responsible for transporting goods from one location to another. As with any industry, trucking is constantly evolving, and it's essential to keep an eye on emerging trends and opportunities. In this chapter, we will discuss the future of trucking and the potential changes that may take place in the coming years.

1. Automation Automation is rapidly making its way into the trucking industry. The development of autonomous trucks promises to revolutionize the industry by eliminating the need for drivers. While fully autonomous trucks are not yet a reality, significant progress has been made, and it is expected that they will soon become a fixture on our roads. This technology will bring benefits such as increased safety, reduced operating costs, and increased efficiency.

2. Electric Trucks Another emerging trend in the trucking industry is the development of electric trucks. With the push for sustainability and

reduced carbon emissions, the development of electric trucks is gaining momentum. Electric trucks have the potential to revolutionize the industry by providing a more environmentally friendly solution to freight transportation. While they are still in the development phase, many manufacturers are investing in electric trucks, and it is expected that they will become more common in the near future.

3. E-Commerce The rise of e-commerce has had a significant impact on the trucking industry. With more people shopping online, there has been a corresponding increase in the demand for trucking services to transport goods. The growth of e-commerce has created new opportunities for trucking companies, and many are expanding their operations to meet the increased demand.

4. Data Analytics Data analytics is an emerging trend in the trucking industry. The use of data analytics can help companies optimize their operations by providing insights into their business processes. With the use of data analytics, companies can make better decisions and improve their overall efficiency.

5. Blockchain Technology Another emerging trend in the trucking industry is the use of blockchain technology. Blockchain technology provides a secure and efficient way to store and transfer data. In the trucking industry, blockchain technology can be used to track the movement of goods, reduce fraud, and increase transparency in the supply chain.

6. Last-Mile Delivery The last mile of the delivery process is one of the most challenging aspects of the trucking industry. The last mile refers to the final stage of the delivery process, from the transportation hub to the end customer. The rise of e-commerce has created new opportunities for last-mile delivery services, and many trucking companies are expanding their operations to include this service.

7. Increased Collaboration Collaboration between trucking companies and other stakeholders in the supply chain is becoming more important. With the rise of e-commerce and the increasing demand for trucking services, it is essential for trucking companies to collaborate with other companies in the supply chain to ensure the smooth and efficient movement of goods.

8. Shift Towards Customer-Centric Approach
   There is a growing trend towards a customer-centric approach in the trucking industry. With the increasing demand for freight transportation, customers are becoming more demanding, and trucking companies must focus on providing a high level of customer service. Companies that adopt a customer-centric approach are more likely to succeed in the industry.

9. Talent Shortage There is currently a talent shortage in the trucking industry, and this is expected to continue in the coming years. As more experienced drivers retire, there are not enough new drivers to fill the gap. This shortage of talent presents a significant challenge for the industry and will require innovative solutions to address.

As we look ahead to the future of the trucking industry, there are a number of emerging trends and opportunities that are likely to shape the way the industry evolves over the coming years. From technological advancements to changes in consumer behavior, there are a variety of factors that will influence the way trucking companies operate and compete in the market.

One of the most significant trends in the industry is the increasing use of technology to optimize operations and improve safety. Advancements in autonomous vehicles, for example, have the potential to revolutionize the trucking industry by making it possible to automate long-haul deliveries and reduce labor costs. While fully autonomous trucks are still a ways off, we are likely to see continued development of semi-autonomous systems that make it easier for drivers to operate their vehicles safely and efficiently.

Another key trend in the industry is the growing demand for sustainability and environmentally-friendly practices. This is driven in part by consumer demand for companies to reduce their carbon footprint, but it is also being pushed by government regulations that are designed to promote sustainability and reduce pollution. As a result, we are likely to see more trucking companies adopt hybrid and electric vehicles, as well as implement strategies for reducing fuel consumption and emissions.

In addition to these technological and environmental trends, there are also a number of emerging opportunities in the trucking industry that companies should be aware of. One of the most significant is the rise of e-commerce, which has created a huge demand for faster and more efficient shipping services. This has led to the growth of last-mile delivery services, which focus on delivering packages directly to consumers' homes or workplaces. As a result, there are many opportunities for trucking companies to partner with e-commerce companies and offer more specialized delivery services.

Another emerging opportunity in the industry is the growth of the sharing economy. This includes the rise of ride-sharing services like Uber and Lyft, as well as the emergence of peer-to-peer truck sharing platforms. These services make it easier for individuals and businesses to rent out their vehicles to others who need them, creating new opportunities for trucking companies to expand their services and reach new customers.

Of course, with all of these emerging trends and opportunities comes a great deal of uncertainty and potential disruption. It's impossible to predict exactly how the industry will evolve over the coming years, but it is clear that companies that are able to adapt quickly and stay ahead of the curve will be in the best position to succeed.

To stay competitive in this rapidly-evolving industry, trucking companies will need to be flexible, innovative, and responsive to the changing needs of their customers. This will require a willingness to invest in new technologies and processes, as well as a commitment to sustainability and other socially responsible practices.

Ultimately, the future of trucking is full of promise and opportunity, but it will also be marked by rapid change and disruption. The companies that are able to navigate these challenges and embrace new opportunities will be the ones that thrive in the years to come.

Chapter 38

Finding Inspiration

The trucking industry has always been one of the most important and fundamental components of the global economy. As a result, there have been many successful entrepreneurs who have made their mark in this industry, and their stories can provide valuable inspiration for those looking to make their own mark. In this chapter, we will explore the success stories of some of the most successful trucking entrepreneurs and their businesses.

1. Max Fuller, CEO of U.S. Xpress Enterprises Max Fuller is the co-founder and CEO of U.S. Xpress Enterprises, one of the largest privately owned trucking companies in the United States. Fuller founded the company in 1985 with a single truck and a vision to create a company that would revolutionize the trucking industry. Over the years, he has used his entrepreneurial spirit and business acumen to grow the company into a $2 billion enterprise.

Fuller's success can be attributed to his ability to innovate and adapt to the changing needs of the industry. For example, he was one of the first trucking executives to embrace new technologies, such as satellite tracking and electronic logging devices, to improve efficiency and safety.

2. Sharon D. Banks, CEO of MVB Trucking Sharon D. Banks is the CEO of MVB Trucking, a company that specializes in hauling high-value cargo, such as fine art and expensive electronics. She founded the company in 2002 after years of working in the trucking industry, and she has built it into a successful business with over 100 employees and a fleet of specialized trucks.

Banks' success can be attributed to her dedication to providing exceptional customer service and her commitment to building a strong team. She has invested heavily in her employees, offering extensive training and education programs, and has created a positive work environment that encourages growth and development.

3. Donald Broughton, Managing Partner of Broughton Capital Donald Broughton is the managing partner of Broughton Capital, a financial research firm that focuses on the transportation industry. He is widely regarded as one of the foremost experts on the trucking industry and has been called upon by major

news outlets and government agencies for his insights.

Broughton's success can be attributed to his unique approach to analyzing the industry. He uses a combination of economic analysis and first-hand experience to provide a comprehensive view of the market, and he is not afraid to challenge conventional wisdom or speak out on controversial issues.

4. Chris Spear, President and CEO of the American Trucking Associations Chris Spear is the president and CEO of the American Trucking Associations, the largest national trade association for the trucking industry. He has been a driving force in advocating for the interests of the industry and has worked tirelessly to promote the importance of trucking to the U.S. economy.

Spear's success can be attributed to his strategic vision and his ability to bring together a diverse group of stakeholders to achieve common goals. He has led successful campaigns to promote the industry and has worked to improve the image of trucking among the general public.

5. Keith Tuttle, President of Motor Carrier Service Keith Tuttle is the president of Motor Carrier

Service, a company that specializes in providing logistical services for the construction industry. He has been a leader in the industry for over 40 years and has built a successful business that provides services to some of the largest construction projects in the country.

Tuttle's success can be attributed to his commitment to providing personalized service to his clients and his ability to adapt to changing market conditions. He has built a loyal customer base by focusing on building strong relationships and providing exceptional service, and he has used his industry knowledge to anticipate and respond to changes in the market.

In conclusion, the trucking industry is a competitive and dynamic field that requires entrepreneurs to be agile, innovative, and forward-thinking. Learning from successful entrepreneurs in the industry can provide valuable insights and inspiration to help you achieve your goals and overcome challenges.

Whether it's implementing new technologies, diversifying your offerings, building effective communication channels, or addressing the driver shortage, there are always new opportunities to improve and grow your business. By staying up-to-date with emerging trends and best practices, and by continually learning from the successes and failures of those who have come before you, you can position yourself for success in the exciting and evolving world of trucking.

So don't be afraid to reach out to industry leaders, attend conferences and events, and connect with other entrepreneurs in the field. By learning from others and applying these insights to your own business, you can achieve your goals, create a strong and resilient business, and make a positive impact on the industry as a whole.

Strategies for Success

Running a successful trucking business can be a challenging endeavor. However, learning from other successful trucking businesses can help you achieve your goals and find the right path to success. Here are some key lessons and best practices from successful trucking businesses that you can adopt to help ensure the success of your own business.

1. Invest in technology Successful trucking businesses understand the importance of investing in technology to improve efficiency, reduce costs, and enhance the customer experience. From GPS tracking to automated scheduling and dispatching systems, investing in technology can help you streamline your operations and stay competitive in a rapidly evolving industry.

2. Prioritize safety Safety should always be a top priority for any trucking business. Successful businesses understand the importance of maintaining their vehicles and investing in safety technology such as lane departure warning systems and collision mitigation

systems. They also prioritize driver training and education to ensure their drivers are equipped with the skills and knowledge necessary to operate their vehicles safely.

3. Focus on customer service Building strong customer relationships is essential to the success of any trucking business. Successful businesses prioritize customer service by providing reliable and on-time deliveries, maintaining open lines of communication with their customers, and going above and beyond to meet their needs. Building a strong reputation for exceptional customer service can help your business stand out in a competitive market and attract new customers.

4. Embrace sustainability The trucking industry has a significant impact on the environment, and successful businesses understand the importance of embracing sustainable practices to reduce their carbon footprint. From investing in fuel-efficient vehicles to implementing sustainable supply chain practices, there are many ways to reduce the environmental impact of your trucking business and appeal to customers who prioritize sustainability.

5. Build a strong team The success of any trucking business is heavily dependent on the quality of its team. Successful businesses understand the importance of recruiting and retaining top talent, offering competitive salaries and benefits, and investing in training and development to help their employees grow and advance in their careers. Building a strong team can help your business deliver exceptional service and achieve long-term success.

6. Monitor industry trends The trucking industry is constantly evolving, and successful businesses stay ahead of the curve by monitoring industry trends and adapting to changes in the market. By staying informed about emerging technologies, regulatory changes, and shifts in consumer preferences, you can position your business to take advantage of new opportunities and stay competitive in a rapidly evolving industry.

7. Stay financially savvy Running a successful trucking business requires sound financial management. Successful businesses understand the importance of budgeting, managing cash flow, and staying on top of accounts payable and receivable. They also invest in financial

planning and analysis to identify areas for cost savings and opportunities for growth.

By adopting these key lessons and best practices from successful trucking businesses, you can position your own business for long-term success. Remember to prioritize safety, customer service, and sustainability, build a strong team, monitor industry trends, and stay financially savvy to ensure the success of your business.

Chapter 40

Making Your Mark

The trucking industry has long been a staple of the global economy, providing essential services to businesses and consumers alike. As the industry continues to evolve and face new challenges, it is essential for trucking businesses to focus on long-term success and growth in order to stay competitive and achieve their goals. This chapter will explore strategies and best practices for achieving success in the trucking industry and positioning your business for sustained growth.

1. Focus on Your Core Competencies

One key strategy for achieving long-term success in the trucking industry is to focus on your core competencies. By identifying the areas in which your business excels and prioritizing these strengths, you can build a competitive advantage and differentiate your business from competitors. This may involve specializing in a particular type of freight or service, such as specialized freight or last-mile delivery, or focusing on a particular region or niche market.

2. Embrace Technology

Technology is transforming the trucking industry, from the use of telematics and GPS tracking to automated vehicles and digital freight matching. To stay competitive and achieve long-term success, it is essential for trucking businesses to embrace these new technologies and incorporate them into their operations. This may involve investing in new hardware and software, partnering with technology providers, or developing in-house expertise.

3. Build Strong Relationships

In the trucking industry, relationships are key. Building strong relationships with customers, shippers, and suppliers can help you win new business, retain existing customers, and improve operational efficiency. This may involve offering personalized service, providing timely and accurate communication, and collaborating with partners to solve problems and optimize supply chains.

4. Prioritize Safety and Compliance

Safety and compliance are essential for any trucking business, and should be a top priority for achieving long-term success. This may involve implementing safety training and policies, using advanced safety technologies, and ensuring compliance with regulations and industry standards. By prioritizing safety and compliance, trucking businesses can protect their drivers and assets, reduce the risk of accidents and incidents, and build a positive reputation in the industry.

5. Focus on Employee Satisfaction and Retention

Employee satisfaction and retention are also critical for achieving long-term success in the trucking industry. Truck drivers and other staff play a vital role in the success of any trucking business, and it is essential to create a positive work environment that values their contributions and provides opportunities for growth and development. This may involve offering competitive compensation and benefits, providing training and professional development opportunities, and fostering a supportive and collaborative work culture.

6. Develop a Long-Term Growth Strategy

Finally, to achieve long-term success and growth in the trucking industry, it is essential to develop a comprehensive growth strategy. This may involve setting clear goals and objectives, identifying potential opportunities for expansion and diversification, and developing a roadmap for achieving these goals over the long term. By focusing on sustainable growth and making strategic investments in people, technology, and operations, trucking businesses can position themselves for success in the years ahead.

Conclusion

The trucking industry is constantly evolving, and achieving long-term success requires a commitment to innovation, growth, and adaptation. By focusing on your core competencies, embracing new technologies, building strong relationships, prioritizing safety and compliance, fostering employee satisfaction and retention, and developing a long-term growth strategy, you can position your trucking business for sustained success and growth in the years ahead. With dedication, hard work, and a willingness to adapt to change, the opportunities for success in the trucking industry are endless.

Thank you for taking the time to read this book on the trucking industry. We hope that it has provided you with valuable insights, tips, and strategies for starting and growing your trucking business.

As you embark on your journey, always remember that success in the trucking industry requires hard work, determination, and a willingness to adapt to changes in the market. By implementing the best practices and lessons shared in this book, you can position your business for long-term success and growth.

We wish you all the best as you take on the exciting and challenging world of trucking. May you find fulfillment, prosperity, and satisfaction in all your endeavors. Good luck!